Command and Communication Frictions in the Gettysburg Campaign

By Philip M. Cole

Colecraft Industries
Since 1981

COLECRAFT INDUSTRIES

Published by Colecraft Industries
970 Mt. Carmel Road
Orrtanna, PA 17353
http: //www.colecraftbooks@aol.com

ISBN 0-9777125-1-6

First edition, first printing.

PRINTED AND BOUND IN THE UNITED STATES OF AMERICA

Contents

Acknowledgments 5

Introduction 6
- Scope 7
- Command and Communications 8

Part One: Command Frictions 9
- Seniority Protocol 9
- Crossing Spheres of Command 13
- Changes in the Chain of Command 17
- Continuity 18
- Changed Style 19
- Personal Relationships 22
- Familiarity 26
- Command Changes: The Domino Effect 29
- Temporary Command Changes from SupportingRoles 32
- Frictions with: Senior Commander on the Field/Wing Commands/Corps Commands 33
- Senior Commander on the Field 33
- Wing Commands 33
- Corps Commands 34
- Arrival of Lesser Commands 38
- Lack of Notification 39
- Command Summary 42

Part Two: Communication Frictions 45
- Protocol 45
- Staff Communication 51
- Communicator Style 58
- Message Origination 60
- Communication Friction Causes 61
- Conflicting Orders 62
- Uncertain Instructions 62
- Insufficient Instructions 63
- Disregarded Orders 65
- Orders with Difficult Prerequisites 69
- Poor or Incorrect Wording 69
- Discretionary Orders 72

Failed Notification 76
Cutoff Communication 77
Encryption Problems 79
Communication Transmission 79
The Human Factor 82
Discipline to Follow Orders 86
Non-Communication 87

Conclusion 88

Bibliography 91

Notes 94

Index 100

ACKNOWLEDGEMENTS

I am fortunate to work with a large group of learned individuals – the licensed battlefield guides and park rangers at the Gettysburg National Military Park. This group holds an immense wealth of knowledge, a variety of opinions, and valuable perspectives about the Gettysburg campaign. I would like to collectively extend my thanks to them for the tidbits of information that helped prepare this work.

A special thanks is due to Paul Clark Cooksey, Licensed Battlefield Guide/author, Dr. Richard Goedkoop, Licensed Battlefield Guide, Jack Wise, Licensed Battlefield Guide, and Eric Campbell, Park Ranger/author/historian. All four have unselfishly devoted many hours reading the manuscript and provided their ideas, suggestions, corrections, and encouragement on this project.

Lastly, I must acknowledge the support of my family, particularly my wife and best friend, Diane, who has shown total patience and understanding in the completion of this work and the continued encouragement from my daughters, Renee and Kerry.

All photographs courtesy of Library of Congress

INTRODUCTION

Prussian military thinker Carl von Clausewitz, widely acknowledged as one of the most important of the major strategic theorists, said:

> Everything is very simple in war, but the simplest thing is difficult. These difficulties accumulate and produce a friction, which no man can imagine exactly who has not seen war….Friction is the only conception which, in a general way, corresponds to that which distinguishes real war from war on paper. The military machine...appears...easy to manage. But let us reflect that no part of it is in one piece...each of which keeps up its own friction in all directions. Theoretically all sounds very well...But it is not so in reality...The danger which war brings with it, the bodily exertions which it requires, augment this evil so much, that they may be regarded as the greatest causes of it. [1]

Von Clausewitz aptly described the uncertainties or "frictions" of war - the mechanisms which complicated warfare. Frictions are the constant streams of obstacles thrown in the way of planning and the governor of progress. Armies encountered any number of unpredictable obstacles in any number of situations. Each friction requires a different solution. Each challenge is a diversion from the planned objective. Each unplanned task saps an army's resources needed elsewhere. Resolution calls for concentrated skills, creative imagination, and improvisation to correct reverses caused by frictions. Solutions, therefore, are more often art than science.

In terms of the Gettysburg campaign, here is one example of a friction: On June 20th, 1863, the Army of the Potomac was preparing to cross the Potomac River into Maryland. Captain Charles Turnbull, commanding engineers, Edwards Ferry, communicated to the army's chief of staff, Gen. Daniel Butterfield:

> Will commence laying the bridge just as soon as possible. It will probably take all night to get the boats into the river. I was ordered here with 60 boats – 1200 feet of bridge. I brought 65 boats. I found on measuring the river the width is 1,400 feet if not over, and immediately telegraphed Gen. Benham for more boats. Since morning the river has risen two feet. Gen. Benham has telegraphed me he would send extra boats at once. They

cannot reach here before tomorrow evening. Will go ahead and do the best I can. [2]

While some students of the battle prefer not to speculate on how much an incident such as the above example affected an outcome, there can be no value placed on the importance of such a friction without at least giving it some consideration. The bridge at Edward's Ferry was the one used by Union units that engaged in the first day's battle at Gettysburg. The delayed crossing postponed the movement of Union forces for an entire day and, quite probably, delayed their arrival at Gettysburg. Had enough bridging been available, it may have allowed the Army of the Potomac to concentrate sooner at Gettysburg and prevented Union troops from being overrun by the superior manpower of Gen. Robert E. Lee's forces.

Frictions are often mentioned in battle reports and narratives, more or less, as incidental information. They are usually detached from any factor that caused defeat or victory. Collectively, though, frictions steered the armies into making major decisions and altering or reversing plans. They drew commanders' attention to less important details in operations at the expense of maintaining balance over the big picture. In the pages to follow it will be shown that frictions had a definite effect in determining the outcomes of battle campaigns.

Scope

There are no greater functions that so affected the operations of an army than the topics of this work - command and communication. Although they have always been considered important in studying historic military events, the frictions associated with these two subjects have not been emphasized enough to associate with and to help analyze their impact.

This work will not be a discussion on techniques of good leadership or communication hardware. It will not be an analysis on how well things went. It will, instead, analyze the frictions that interfered with or otherwise tested the greatness of commanders, uncovered the weaknesses of systems, and challenged the skills of communicators. The focus is on one campaign, Gettysburg.

Command and communication frictions affected many important actions in the Gettysburg story: They altered Lee's original plan to move towards Harrisburg, Pennsylvania and diverted the Army of Northern Virginia to Gettysburg; they caused forward elements of the

Confederate army to provoke a general engagement against Lee's instructions. In the Army of the Potomac, they caused a great deal of confusion in recognizing who was in charge at any one time or place. Even though this study concentrates on frictions in the Gettysburg campaign, the revelations from this one operation, nevertheless, can be applied to any battle of any war.

This work uses a variety of incidents, some familiar, to illustrate their serious impact on the battle – at least as much as troops in combat affected the outcome. The incidents used are in no way meant to portray any individual as incompetent, nor does it question anyone's commitment. Illustrations used merely portray humans, imperfect as we all are, working with an imperfect system, during severe conditions of physical and mental stress. The examples presented deal mainly with the high commands of the armies, especially the Army of the Potomac. The high command level was where the most important decisions were made to influence the progress of the army and the destiny its troops.

Command and Communication

The roles of command and communication were the centerpieces which allowed Civil War armies to operate. They have always been and always will be interdependent. A good leader with poor communications was no better than a bad leader with good communications. Both must perform equally well to fulfill a mission.

The functions of command and communication allowed information to be transferred and digested in order to develop operations. Command and communication permitted armies to realign forces - to respond to threats or take advantage of new opportunities. Commanders lead their forces with plans, plans were converted to orders, and orders were communicated to subordinates. Subordinates, in turn, communicated information to superiors and superiors made plans to convert this information to orders, completing the cycle of the command/communication relationship.

Part One: Command Frictions

The implementation of command and communication was done through the *chain of command.* The chain of command is defined as "a system whereby authority passes down from the top through a series of executive positions or military ranks in which each is accountable to the one directly superior." Each subordinate, therefore, must acknowledge that his direct superior is in charge. In today's American army, many agree that the "implementation of the chain of command is the most important strategy employed by our military forces. In other armies the loss of a commander would throw the entire organization into disorder while in the U. S. military, the next most senior person present just assumes command. It is taught that whenever two Marines are walking together, one is in charge." [3]

On paper, a chain of command is a design with defined paths for orders or information to flow. This chain displays the hierarchy of commander and subordinate. It can distinguish between units which are directly controlled by a specific commander and administratively controlled by another commander. In both armies, for example, front line artillery units were commanded by infantry commanders responsible for the sector in which they were located, but administratively controlled by the chiefs of artillery.

When all subordinates in the chain of command knew whose orders they were to obey and when all superiors knew who were to obey their orders, the frictions affecting control were greatly diminished and the system worked. While this system was sensible and a good guideline, it relied on protocols which could vary and, consequently, it put pre-established order out of balance. Von Clausewitz's observations that "...the simplest thing is difficult," and " these difficulties accumulate and produce a friction," become apparent when reality tested the system.

Seniority Protocol

The method used to fill vacancies in command was replacement by seniority, based on date of appointment. Using seniority was a routine procedure and the most important determination in promotion. Many officers knew their peers' dates of appointment to rank, knew their place in the seniority lineup, and expected to rise in position accordingly.

Chain of Command Illustration (Army of the Potomac's 1st Corps)

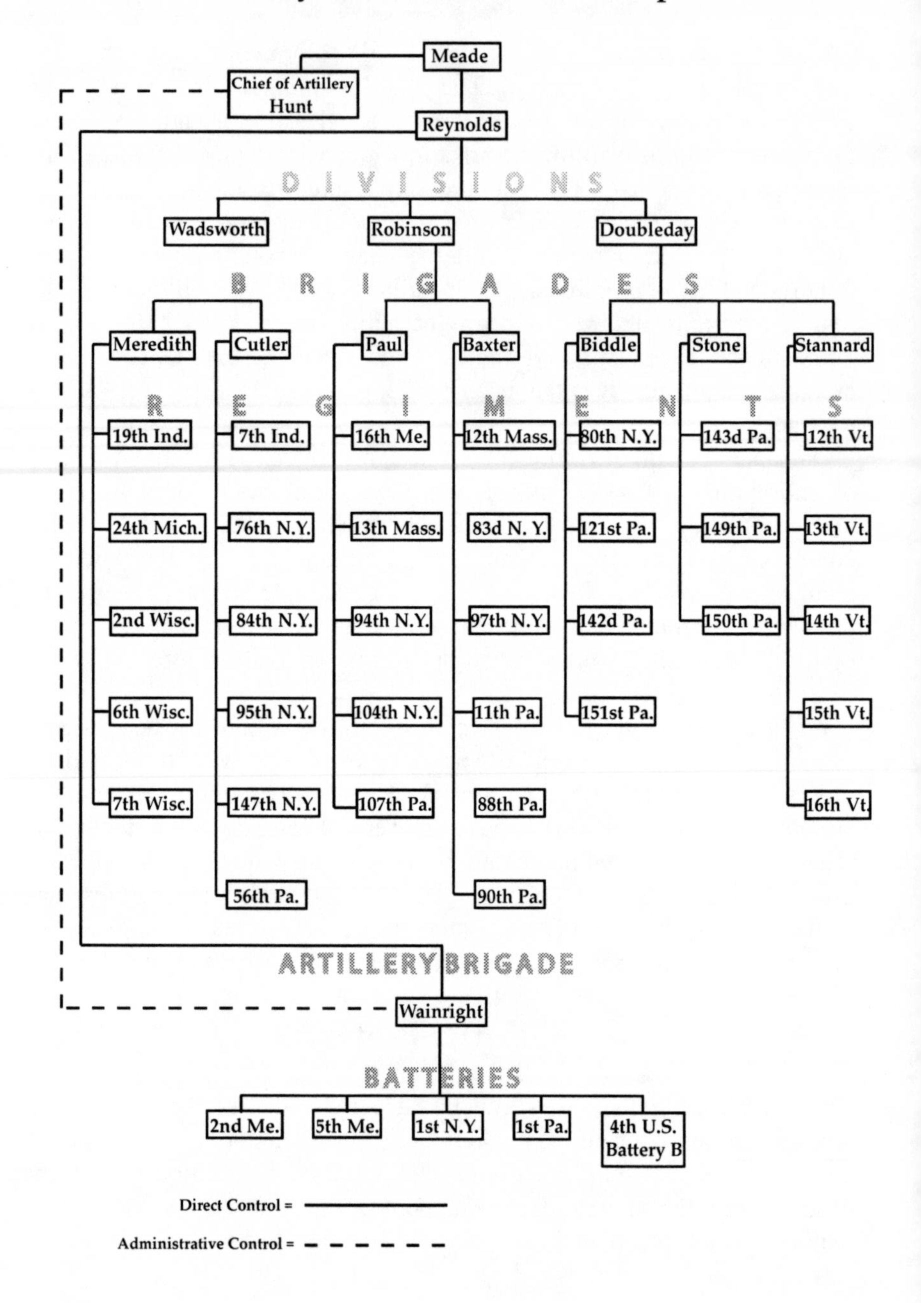

Promotion by seniority was the method used mostly, but not totally. When exceptions were made, officers were naturally offended when junior officers were promoted over them. Consequently, commanders with seniority were highly sensitive to taking orders from officers, comparable in rank, but junior in date of appointment. Conversely, some commanders with junior appointment dates were equally sensitive to giving orders to subordinates senior to them.

From an outsider's view, sensitivity to the seniority issue, especially during an invasion crisis, seemed trivial and that such matters would be ignored over more important concerns. However, just five days before the battle of Gettysburg, Gen. Joseph Hooker, then commanding the Army of the Potomac, took time to deal with a seniority problem. He sent an appeal to Secretary of War, Edwin Stanton: "I would respectfully request that Major-General [Julius] Stahel [Division cavalry commander in Heintzelman's military department] may be ordered by telegraph to report to General Couch, with a view to organizing and putting in an efficient condition any mounted troops that can be raised for service there. His presence here as senior major-general will much embarrass me and retard my movements." Stanton replied, "Major-General Stahel is relieved from duty in the Army of the Potomac, and will report to General Couch, at Harrisburg, to organize and command the cavalry in the Department of the Susquehanna." [4]

Perhaps there were other reasons, not expressed in Hooker's request, for Stahel's removal. On the surface, however, seniority seemed more important to Gen. Hooker than having the assistance of an experienced officer [a future Medal of Honor recipient] in a time of extreme crisis. Even though Hooker's passage through another's military district was temporary, he was willing to "banish" an officer who had expertise and knowledge of the countryside in order to claim senior status.

After the battle of Gettysburg, the Army of the Potomac, then commanded by Gen. George Meade, faced the same chain of command and seniority problems as those experienced by Gen. Hooker. Meade was moving back to Virginia. He was re-assigning commanders for troops stationed in the military district he was leaving. In one assignment he stated that he would "...be separated from communications with Harper's Ferry, I request that you [Gen. Darius Couch] will assume command of the troops at Maryland Heights and vicinity. These troops number about 4,000 men, and, are under the command of Brigadier-General Henry Lockwood, who has been directed to look to you for further instructions..." [5]

It is unclear why Meade would appoint Couch over troops at Maryland Heights and vicinity. This area was in a military department commanded by Gen. Robert Schenck while Couch currently commanded the Department of the Susquehanna, not even close to Maryland Heights. In any event, in executing his new assignment, Couch placed Gen. W. F. Smith, U.S. Volunteers, in charge of all troops in Maryland. This command included the whole of Gen. Lockwood's forces; however, Smith, in his new command, was junior to the now subordinate, Lockwood.

In the course of business Smith required from Lockwood a report on his depots and their condition. Lockwood, thinking Smith was mistakenly assigned to be his superior, appealed to Gen. Schenck, department commander: "It gives me pleasure, as a matter of courtesy, to render the foregoing information [the required depot report]; but presuming that General Couch had no intention of placing me under the orders of a junior, I reply only through courtesy. Besides this, Major-General Schenck notifies me that he claims jurisdiction over my command, and expects me to obey his orders." At this point, their superior, Gen. Henry Halleck, General-in-Chief of the Army, intervened and sent a message to both Schenck and Lockwood to sort out the confusion: "...So long as military operations continue on the Potomac, all troops in the field, no matter what department they belong, are under the orders of General Meade." [6]

But the confusion in the prevailing chain of command did not end there. Lockwood responded to Halleck: "When General Meade left Berlin, he directed me to report to General Couch, commanding Department of the Susquehanna. I did. Subsequently General Schenck claimed authority over me, and directed me to report to him. This morning an order came from General Couch, placing me under the orders of General W.F. Smith, who is my junior, and General Smith sends me an order to report number, position, and condition to him. Of course I cannot obey Smith's order unless by special assignment. Please settle this matter." Halleck contacted Couch: "If you wish General Smith to command at Harper's Ferry, General Lockwood should be relieved. You have no authority, so far as I am aware, to place a junior officer over a senior." [7]

The confusion from this friction - a blurred chain of command - and how it affected the disposition and movement of troops at critical moments is remarkable. With better staff work to prevent oversights such as this and greater care in communicating, the confusion appears to have been largely preventable. The Army of Northern Virginia, on the other hand, when operating in enemy territory, did not have jurisdictional problems with friendly units from other military departments and was unbothered by such diversions.

Crossing Spheres of Commands

Lee's move northward faced a number of problems special only to the Army of Northern Virginia. The army was leaving its home ground; it was decreasing the protection of Richmond and, at the same time, losing access to quick reinforcement; it was crossing regions of the country occupied by citizens with mixed allegiances and heading into country hostile to the Southern cause. The further north the Confederate army moved, lines of communication lengthened and communication transmission time increased; links were constricted to narrow corridors of control, vulnerable to severing. In the process, Lee's manpower was slowly evaporating to guard the extended lines of communications and supply links to home ground.

Conversely, as Gen. Hooker's army moved northward, shadowing Lee's line of march, he gained all the advantages that Lee was losing. The Army of the Potomac was moving into friendly territory and gaining easier access to supplies. Lines of communication were shrinking, speeding up communications, and freeing up soldiers who guarded the lines.

Additionally, by moving northward, Hooker's army grew in strength by adding troops from other military departments. The accretion of men from other sources, however, introduced complications. The Army of the Potomac was entering space controlled by other commanders. In maneuvering to the movements of Confederate forces, it would brush by or pass over territory protected by military departments with fixed geographic areas and outside of Hooker's control. To counter the Confederate army's movements, however, all available resources were needed to unite and act in concert against Lee as his army approached and crossed through the respective Federal military departments or *spheres of command.*

The additional local troops assisting the Army of the Potomac included three military districts. They would, according to circumstance, support, reinforce, be absorbed into, or intermingle with other commands outside their normal assignments. The districts included the Department of Washington, which covered Harper's y, Maj. Gen. Samuel Heintzelman commanding, the Middle Military Department headquartered in Baltimore, Maj. Gen. Robert Schenck, commanding, and the Department of the Susquehanna headquartered in Harrisburg, Maj. Gen. Darius Couch, commanding.

As both armies pressed northward, the tension was building for a probable engagement. The Army of the Potomac was passing through military departments outside of Hooker's traditional control. The difficulty in maintaining a clear chain of command increased as additional units within those territories were absorbed into Hooker's force and entered into joint operations. Units, pulled from the military departments, now had a different commanding-general; and, in the process of transferring power, the chain of command was again blurred by command frictions.

Temporarily restructuring the chain of command could work if certain considerations were attended to: 1. Only one person could act as commanding-general to coordinate operations during an exceedingly fluid situation; 2. The commanding-general must have a clear understanding as to which forces were "loaned" for his use; 3. He must know their disposition and troop strength [Hooker was not up to speed as to their troop strengths or dispositions]; 4. Information on the restructured chain of command must be quickly promulgated within the Army of the Potomac and the military districts participating; 5. Hooker, operating outside his traditional assigned area, and the military departments' commanders-in-chief must act cooperatively and in unison.

Since the Army of the Potomac would be the chief combatant when the fighting started, it was obvious that its commanding-general should take control. On June 22nd, Gen. Halleck offered Gen. Hooker assistance by suggesting that more troops be added to his command, "In order to give compactness to the command of troops in the field covering Washington and Baltimore, it is proposed to place that part of the Middle Department east of Cumberland, now commanded by General Schenck, under your direct orders." [Some units attached to two of the three military districts, Schenck's and Heintzelman's, were already under Hooker's control.] Hooker responded, "I have to state yes, provided that the same authority is continued to me that I now have, which is to give orders direct to the troops in the departments of Generals Schenck and Heintzelman."

Halleck gave Hooker the requested authority. He said, "General Schenck has been notified that the troops of his department in Harper's Ferry and vicinity would obey all orders direct from you, and that he would obey your orders in regard to the other troops of his command." Hooker sent his chief-of-staff to Washington and Baltimore to ascertain the troop dispositions and strengths of those departments. While this was happening, Gen. Hooker issued orders to his newly assigned troops within the departments.

Although the temporary chain of command was established, the system was quickly beginning to run into problems in recognizing who was in charge. This command friction was brought on by two commands operating in the same space. On June 25, Hooker was made aware of a dispatch sent by Gen. Samuel Crawford, division commander, Army of the Potomac. Crawford said, "A dispatch has been received during the night from General [John] Slough, military governor of Alexandria, informing me that the commanding officer of the Second Brigade, Pennsylvania Reserve Corps, has been instructed by him not to recognize the orders sent to him to prepare to join the division, as directed in your dispatch of June 23."

In response, Hooker requested that Halleck punish Slough: "I request that General Slough be arrested at once, and charges will be forwarded as soon as I have time to prepare them. You will find, I fear, when it is too late, that the effort to preserve department lines will be fatal to the cause of the country." Halleck responded, "The Second Brigade, to which you refer in your telegram, forms no part of General Crawford's command, which was placed at your orders. No other troops can be withdrawn from the Defenses of Washington."

In another situation, Hooker communicated to Halleck: "...I desire that instructions may be given Generals Heintzelman and Schenck to direct their commands to obey promptly any orders they may receive from me. Last evening the colonel commanding at Poolesville responded to his orders to march that he did not belong to my command, but would refer his orders to General Heintzelman. Such delays may bring us reverses. When these instructions are given, I shall not be necessitated to repeat orders to any part of my command to march on the enemy." Hooker's despair over the frictions of command and control was evident when he added, "I request that my orders be sent me to-day, for outside of the Army of the Potomac I don't know whether I am standing on my head or feet." [8]

Either Washington did not inform Hooker as to what troops were available to him or his staff did not ascertain this information. Hooker's focus should have been riveted on what Lee was doing and not having to spend time on matters deemed administrative. He could little afford to address internal problems from subordinate commanders, supposedly newly assigned to his command, who rejected his orders. Hooker used up precious time communicating to others in order to establish his authority. Such command problems did not have to be.

While the above examples happened on a strategic level, the effects of command frictions caused from crossing spheres of command were just as serious in affecting units on a tactical level. In fact, the effects were more immediate and significant in deciding a battle's outcome. At Gettysburg, this was so true, especially for the Army of the Potomac. With Gen. Meade in command, Union forces spent practically the entire battle in a state of motion. From the beginning of the battle until the end, hardly a unit remained in a stationary position. Units either retreated from their original position, advanced from their assigned position, or were sent to reinforce or support other parts of the line. Most of the shifting forces transited along the battle front laterally, across other spheres of command. Any units crossing over terrain assigned to other commanders who were superior in rank were subject to the whims of those officers.

Consequently, units were snatched up in transit by desperate commanders seeking assistance, irregardless of any dire need for help at their intended destination. Others were slowed down, stopped, or otherwise prevented from attending to emergencies elsewhere. Lt. G. G. Benedict, Vermont Brigade, said, "[The brigade] succeeded only in reaching the ground as the last guns were fired from Cemetery Hill [July 1st]. It marched in on the left, over ground which was occupied by the enemy the next morning, and after some marching and counter-marching, under contradictory orders from different corps commanders, three of whom assumed immediate command of the Brigade, was allowed to halt and drop to rest on the left of Cemetery Hill." [9]

In another instance, Lieutenant Colonel Adolphus Dobke, 45th N.Y. Infantry, 11th Corps reported:

> ....In the evening [July 2nd], at dark, a sudden attack was made on the Twelfth Corps, on our right, and the Forty-fifth Regiment ordered to support. For a mile through the complete darkness in the woods this regiment pushed up to the stone fence through an incessant shower of bullets, and shared well in the defense of this position [Culp's Hill]. It is to be mentioned that while the regiment marched in the darkness through the woods, under guide of a staff officer, the march

> was considerably delayed by a number of general staff officers, each exerting himself to give his orders, and so, by movements, counter-movements, halts, &c., some time elapsed before the regiment found itself in the right place behind the fence.... [10]

Still another example, Captain A. P. Martin, commanding artillery brigade, 5th Corps reported:

> [July 2nd] "Battery C, Massachusetts Artillery, and I, Fifth U.S. Artillery, were left in the rear of the line of battle of the First Division, with instructions to await orders. When positions had been selected and orders sent for the batteries to move to the front, they were not to be found. Subsequently, Battery C, Massachusetts Artillery, was found in the rear of the Third Corps. The officer commanding reported that he had been ordered there by an officer of General Sickles' staff, who had orders to take any batteries he could find, no matter where they belonged. Battery I, Fifth U.S. Artillery, was taken in the same way, thus depriving the Fifth Corps of its proper amount of artillery. [11]

Changes in the Chain of Command

Command adjustments, especially during the Civil War, were frequent and constant. Some changes were temporary adjustments made to fill vacancies for officers who were convalescing from recent battles, on leave, or attending duties elsewhere. Some were permanent changes, mostly from combat. Battle losses were expected and inevitable, but were abrupt and unforeseen. Consequently, continual campaigning diminished the army of experienced and skilled leaders - resources which could not be recovered quickly.

Command changes, even in cases where better officers replaced less effective ones, were, nevertheless, disruptive in the flow of operations: they severed familiar links of communication, they interrupted leadership continuity during critical moments, they caused orders to be challenged by anyone not notified of the command change, and they disrupted continuity between commander and subordinate.

Continuity

Continuity of leadership in any organization was important. Constancy created stability. Stability preserved relationships. Familiarity of personnel within an organization, even if subordinates and superiors did not get along, at the very least provided a level of understanding with which to interact.

Conversely, lost continuity from command changes was accompanied with a degree of caution between commander and subordinate and a sense of the unknown. The dynamics of communications were altered, working relationships ended, and old alliances, formed between superior and subordinate, were exchanged for those yet to be formed. Even if subordinates knew replacement commanders from working with them in a lesser role, new positions called for different relationships. Former acquaintances were now either peers, subordinates or superior officers.

The replacement of Gen. Hooker by George Meade gives us a powerful example of fracturing the chain of command and breaking the continuity of leadership. The change was abrupt and unforeseen and happened just three days before the battle of Gettysburg. Meade received his promotion unexpectedly. He was untested in the role of army commander. The transition was an overwhelming challenge - adjusting from leading his former command, the 5th Corps, of 13,000 to controlling an entire army with a force approaching 100,000. [12]

For Meade, the timing could not have been worse. Meade had three days before the battle of Gettysburg to study the military situation – not as a corps commander, but as a commanding-general. Before he could come up with any plan or positioning of troops, he had to learn what resources he had available; he was not familiar with the strengths and weaknesses of all units now in his charge; he had to prepare for an engagement that seemed unavoidable.

With the army in motion, command transition was especially difficult. Gen. Hooker had already established a rhythm of countermoves against those made by the Army of Northern Virginia. To maintain continuity, it was critical for Gen. Hooker to brief Meade on the state of affairs and for the new commanding-general to receive counsel from his corps commanders. Hooker, however, in the meeting transferring the command, gave Meade no intimation of any plan he was considering nor any views he held. In addition, Meade's cavalry and seven infantry corps commanders were scattered over wide areas of the countryside and could not assemble to share their views and current intelligence. [The first time Meade met with them as a group was at the end of the second day's battle at Gettysburg. By then, two of the seven infantry commanders had been killed or wounded.] [13]

Besides breaking command continuity from Hooker's departure, Meade also lost staff continuity by losing the men who assisted him in commanding the 5th Corps. If he had the time, he probably would have preferred creating his commanding-general's staff using officers with which he had an already established working relationship. Instead, Meade inherited Hooker's handpicked men. Although it broke connectivity, keeping Hooker's staff was, undoubtedly, the most beneficial arrangement. Members of that staff were the only ones who knew the big picture and able to maintain continuity in the operation - the general state of affairs, the status of existing orders, the level of supplies, the deployment and availability of forces, and the fighting condition of units.

Comparatively, the Army of Northern Virginia lost command continuity as well. Before the army moved to start the Gettysburg campaign, major modifications in the chain of command occurred. Gen. Lee re-arranged his army from two large infantry corps into three smaller ones. In addition, other Confederate forces were pulled from outside regions and added to the rolls of the Army of Northern Virginia. Consequently, the command continuity of both armies was broken. New relationships and new styles of command were introduced, and, in turn, added to the frictions of command.

Changed Style

Breaking continuity of command also meant changes in leadership style. Style changes disrupted working relationships between persons accustomed to the thought and behavior patterns of others as well as an understanding of others' expectations and limitations. Severed relationships changed routines of operating. The standards demanded by a former commander were not identical to those of his replacement. Meade, for example, was suddenly operating an army imprinted with Hooker's style.

The command styles of Hooker, Meade, and Lee were strikingly different. Gen. Hooker's style practiced one of caution. He shared his plans in a general way without communicating details to his subordinates. Gen. Meade, when he was still a corps commander, wrote his wife about Hooker's style: "[He] is remarkably reticent of his information and plans; I really know nothing of what he intends to do, or when or where he proposes doing anything....[Secrecy] may be carried too far, and important plans may be frustrated by subordinates, from their ignorance of how much depended on their share of work." Gen. Hooker's style suppressed the exchange of important information central to any plans. Consequently, in order to implement the wishes of the commanding-general, actions depended solely on blind loyalty and ignored any valuable input from subordinates, ignorant of details in plans. This deficiency inevitably led to trouble.

Meade's style, as commanding-general, on the other hand, was the opposite of Hooker's. He shared information with his corps commanders by informing them of the latest military situation, he advised them of what his short-term plans were, he treated them more like equals than as subordinates, he sought cooperation and advice from them, and his plans were influenced by their views.

In his Gettysburg strategy, Meade felt inclined to take a defensive approach, thinking his "chances of success were greater in a defensive battle than an offensive one." Preservation of the army and the defense of Northern soil were central to the strategic thinking of the Army of the Potomac's previous commanding-generals. Meade's way of thinking was no exception. Tactically, Meade preferred to remain active along a battle line but detached from front line action; he felt it was better not to observe action firsthand because it shifted the commanding-general's attention towards micromanaging situations at the expense of understanding the overall state of the battle. [14]

Col. E. P. Alexander, Confederate artillery battalion commander, praised Meade's command skill when Gen. Daniel Sickles' 3rd Corps moved away from the Union line on July 2nd: "Meade saw the danger, and with military foresight prepared to meet it with every available man. There was not during the war a finer example of efficient command than that displayed by Meade on this occasion. He immediately began to bring to the scene re-enforcements, both of infantry and artillery, from every corps and every part of the line...He engaged, or in hand on the field, fully 40,000 men by the time that Longstreet's assault was repulsed." [15]

Gen. Lee also had his own style of leadership. Compared to the quick-tempered disposition of Meade, his demeanor was that of a consummate gentleman. Maj. Justus Scheibert of the Prussian Royal Engineers and "a distinguished foreigner who witnessed the battle of Gettysburg," described his admiration for Lee and detailed his attributes which gained his reputation as a great leader:

> Lee was, in my opinion, one of the ablest leaders of this century in two great qualities. He weighed everything, even the smallest detail, in making his general plan of battle, and he made the boldest dispositions with heroic courage and the most stubborn energy. He gave to every link the right place in the construction of a chain which became a masterpiece of military workmanship.
>
> He did not reach his conclusions, as Jackson and Stuart did, by an instinctive, sudden impulse; his plans did not come upon him like the lightning's flash followed by the thunder's crash: but he painfully and studiously labored in order to arrange those splendid dispositions fraught with the keenest and most hardy enterprises, and well worthy of the troops which were ordered to execute them. [16]

Lee knew what he wanted. He did not take votes on issues or seek consensus in formulating his battle plans. He, like Meade, however, listened to subordinates and altered plans from their advice. On July 2nd, for example, he acceded to Gen. Richard Ewell who was against using his 2nd Corps as the main force for an attack on his front and also Lee's alternate suggestion for the corps to move to the right. And then again, on July 3rd, he consented to Longstreet's request not to use two of his exhausted divisions in continuing the attack.

Lee's signature style was one which tended to give orders that were general in nature, not one of micromanagement. His philosophy, in his own self-description, was to provide subordinates with the best opportunities to succeed but they, with their troops, had the tactical responsibility to bring the engagement to a triumphant conclusion. Once the action started he let the battle unfold leaving his subordinate commanders to control the situation. After discussing and finalizing the plan in detail with his commanders, it was left up to them to implement the proposal in their own fashion and arrange any refinements needed to address the nuances and subtleties affecting their battle ground. Lee might sit on a log while the battle unfolded, shunning any effort to "tweak" the operation that tempted other commanders-in-chief and which sometimes interfered with carrying out the plan. [17]

Besides his military genius, Lee's greatest asset as a commanding-general, unrivaled by any other on either side, was his charismatic character – an attribute that cannot be taught. With this trait, Lee motivated his army to perform spectacular accomplishments. In his reminiscences, Confederate General John Gordon pointed out the power of such an asset:

> The respect held by Lee, openly expressed by his men, allowed Lee to proceed with operations fairly free from the customary grumblings of subordinate officers that accompanied the Federal commanders who seemed to perpetually change from one lost battle to the next. Respect, however, suppressed constructive criticism. Lee might blame himself for one failure or another, but any expression of faultfinding towards him by others would have triggered resounding anger and wholesale condemnation. [18]

Personal Relationships

It is human nature, in any setting, that there are conflicting relationships within groups of people. The military is no different. Different types of relationships produced different results; consequently, relationships between commanders and subordinates affected the progress of operations. A stern commander, not respected by subordinates, for example, who issued instructions more as a mechanical process or communicated in an abrasive manner, may have prodded his subordinates to obey his wishes, but responding to orders was probably done with less commitment than those that willingly followed orders from a trusted leader. On the other hand, subordinates, who held the greatest respect for their commanders and confidence that they were always right, may have suppressed opinions or advice that could have helped make better decisions.

And so it was that some officers detested their superiors or vice versa; but, under the pressure of combat, they had to deal with each other, take or give orders, take or give advice, and put aside animosities. Negative personal opinions and combative relationships did not belong in the charged atmosphere of battle where tens of thousands of men relied on their leaders, performing their mission, to act in their best interests.

The relationship between Gen. Hooker and his superiors in Washington illustrates a command friction at the highest level and the poisonous effects of disharmony cast upon an army operation. After an embarrassing defeat at Chancellorsville in May, 1863, Hooker lost the trust of his superiors. He suffered especially from a poor relationship with his immediate superior in Washington, Gen. Halleck. Hooker was under intense pressure from Washington to stop Lee's northward moves.

He needed a morale booster, encouragement and support from his superiors. On June 16th, instead of uplifting advice, Hooker received a barrage of directives that nettled and isolated him, a commander in need of assurance.

During that annoying day Gen. Hooker sent Secretary of War Stanton a simple request: "If General [George] Cadwalader has gone to Pennsylvania, please request him to send me information of the rebel movements to the south of there." Stanton replied, "General Cadwalader has not gone to Pennsylvania, but is here waiting for orders. You shall be kept posted upon all information received here as to enemy's movements, but must exercise your own judgment as to its credibility. The very demon of lying seems to be about these times, and generals will have to be broken for ignorance before they will take the trouble to find out the truth of reports." [19]

Gen. Hooker's sense of helplessness in dealing with Gen. Halleck was revealed in a message to President Lincoln: "You have long been aware, Mr. President, that I have not enjoyed the confidence of the major-general commanding the army, and I can assure you so long as this continues we may look in vain for success, especially as future operations will require our relations to be more dependent upon each other than heretofore." In this same message, Hooker attempted to use Lincoln as an intermediary instead of working with Halleck direct. Hooker suggested possible movements for the Army of the Potomac and stated to Lincoln that if he agreed, to "please let instructions to that effect be given me." The President, however, was not about to circumvent the chain of command. Later that day Lincoln responded to Hooker: "To remove all misunderstanding, I now place you in the strict military relation to General Halleck of a commander of one of the armies to the general-in-chief of all the armies. I have not intended differently, but as it seems to be differently understood, I shall direct him to give you orders and you to obey them."

The abrasive relationship with Halleck and Lincoln's rebuff to mediate, stopped Gen. Hooker from seeking any support and advice from his Washington superiors. Every suggestion he offered them regarding countermoves against Lee's army was rejected. When Gen. Hermann Haupt inquired about his next maneuver, Hooker said he would move nowhere without orders to do so, he would follow instructions literally, and let the blame fall where it belonged. Hooker was already a defeated commander before the battle began. His self-confidence was deflated, his drive and aggressiveness in crushing Lee's army had vanished. [20]

Abrasive relationships affecting communication and operational decisions between commander and subordinate cannot be measured. It can at least be said, however, that such a condition did lend itself to suppressing communications, not reporting true conditions, "feeding" information in a way to avoid censure, or simply giving in and blindly following suggestions from superiors without efforts to correct any flawed assumptions they may have possessed.

Gen. Hooker's rapid departure from his commanding-general's post, without sharing any plans or views of the operation with Meade, exemplifies the action of a man drained and withdrawn by the frustrations from an unworkable relationship between superior and subordinate. [Gen. Halleck took the last stab at the former commanding-general after Gen. Hooker arrived in Washington to see if he could be of any use. Halleck ordered his arrest for visiting the capital without a pass. Lincoln must have interceded since no effort to prosecute him was made.]

Gen. Meade had less baggage in dealing with others than his predecessor. Although many welcomed Meade's promotion as the Army of the Potomac's commanding-general, some regretted Hooker's departure and the timing was unfortunate. According to Col. Regis DeTrobriand, 3rd corps brigade commander, Meade's elevation created resentment, "more or less secret," among some corps commanders. Before Meade's elevation, other corps commanders were Meade's equals; now they were his subordinates. Meade's reputation, however, was one of respect and steadfastness. [21]

Additionally, Meade's relationship with his superiors in Washington quickly soured soon after the victory at Gettysburg. As the Army of the Potomac followed Lee's force southward, Meade received from Washington the same critical treatment in communiqués as Hooker had received before the battle. Although Meade's activity regarding the speed of his pursuit is still debated today, the point to be made is that Meade was so disturbed by the tone of the messages that he threatened to resign.

The leadership in Washington, especially Gen. Halleck, irritated Meade. From Meade's perspective, his superiors had no idea what the Army of the Potomac had just gone through. With the Army of the Potomac's battle losses, it wasn't immediately obvious, even to Meade, who had won; his army was turned inside out, he lost many of his top commanders, the weather turned miserable, but Washington "knew better" than Meade, since Halleck and others had such a clear view of the event from eighty miles away.

The messages from Washington urged Meade to vigorously pursue the enemy and make it suffer. Halleck communicated to Meade: "The opportunity to attack his divided forces should not be lost. The President is urgent and anxious that your army should move against him by forced marches." Meade responded: "My army is and has been making forced marches, short of rations, and barefooted." The apparent lack of understanding by Meade's superiors in Washington presented the commanding-general with an invitation to accede to their views, ignore his own, and make foolish moves to the detriment of his men.

Upon Lee's successful crossing of the Potomac, Halleck communicated to Meade: "I need hardly say to you that the escape of Lee's army without another battle has created great dissatisfaction in the mind of the President, and it will require an active and energetic pursuit on your part to remove the impression that it has not been sufficiently active heretofore." Meade had had enough. Within ninety minutes of this message, Meade responded: "Having performed my duty conscientiously and to the best of my ability, the censure of the President conveyed in your dispatch...is, in my judgment, so undeserved that I feel compelled most respectfully to ask to be immediately relieved from the command of this army." Perhaps Meade's testy relationship with Washington was partially due to dealing with the stigma attached to the sins of caution committed by previous commanding-generals of the Army of the Potomac. [22]

Other commanding-generals' relationships with their superiors fared better under similar circumstances. Even Gen. Lee did not follow up after every one of his victories. Fredericksburg is one example, and he received no grief. In fact, the tone of communications between Gen. Lee and Richmond was always most cordial and gentlemanly. Such interactions never hinted at a level deemed abrasive as those conversations experienced by their northern counterparts.

Since commanders used others as emissaries to convey orders or as extensions of their authority, it was important for these representatives to maintain good relationships within the chain of command. The majority of communications from commanding officers were accomplished through the use of staff officers or aides-de-camp. Some had the authority to make important decisions. Engineering staff officers, for example, were specialists in choosing proper ground to occupy, artillery staff officers were skilled in placing gun batteries.

Since aides were often junior in rank to superior officers to which the orders were directed, a positive relationship was essential for staff or aides to communicate verbal orders to superior officers. With a positive relationship, messengers could express a sense of urgency on behalf of their commander yet not appear to be talking down to a superior officer or be subjected to the "kill the messenger" syndrome.

For officers, lower in the chain of command, however, there was a general animosity and envy towards staff officers and aides-de-camp. They were resented for their rapid advancement by sometimes using family influence to obtain a soft position outright instead of working up the traditional ladder of promotion. They were envied for their open access to the general, for working close to the excitement surrounding a headquarters command, and privy to information denied to others, superior in rank. Especially gritting to officers, excluded from access to the "higher ups," was the display of self-importance which affected some of these "chosen" young aides. Some "rebs" called them "yellow sheep-killing dogs." When aides happened to ride by, soldiers would ridicule them with whistles and imitations of calling hounds. On the other hand, most aides were levelheaded appointees who, nevertheless, suffered the same derision despite the fact that many, as reflected in numerous after-action reports, performed exceptional and heroic deeds at the most dangerous places on a battlefield. [23]

But even positive relationships had a downside to communications. A headquarters command, surrounded by staff and aides who were also friends and relatives eager to assist their leader, created a family atmosphere but it affected the quality of communication [Meade, for example, used his own son as an aide at Gettysburg]. The relationship altered important information to which a commander should be informed. Friends and relatives were likely to shield their beloved commander from outside criticism. Such criticism could contain suggestions and ideas overlooked in the commander's decision-making process. In planning operations, it did a general no good to hear praise on the brilliance of his ideas from a supportive group, absent of legitimate criticism, and leaving the commander with a sense of infallibility.

Familiarity

Familiarity with a commander's style affected the way orders were interpreted and understood by others. Undoubtedly, in the charged atmosphere of a battle it was better to plan and make decisions with a team that held nurtured relationships than to strategize with a group of strangers or even acquaintances unused to working together in a new capacity.

Time was the critical element in building relationships within a command. One of the most powerful forms of bonding was collaborating as a team to perform tasks. Relationships were formed through interactions: conversing, exchanging ideas, sharing advice, or critiquing. Other than known reputations, there were no shortcuts for new commanders to bond and gain the respect, trust, confidence, and cooperation of their men. Time was needed to set personal examples, for commanders to communicate what was expected from subordinates, and to create an atmosphere which elicited honest answers and willing obedience.

Formed relationships established intuitive ability—the natural intelligence to understand things without having to lay out all the details. "Reading" a leader's mind to discern his intentions was an acquired process and not automatically transferred when a new commander took over. Intuition, created from formed relationships, was an invisible communications system which provided the knowledge to know what actions were needed. Prior to Gettysburg, the familiar relationship between Lee and his two infantry corps commanders, Jackson and Longstreet, is often used as a model for the intuitive rapport that existed in this trio of generals. Lee gave directives to his two corps commanders, using minimum details, and they were able to sense what Lee wanted.

Unfamiliarity within a group, on the other hand, characteristically held back honest opinions. In an unfamiliar atmosphere, subordinates were less likely to object to a superior's ideas or give frank advice. [It is interesting to note that some of Meade's subordinate commanders, who were unfamiliar with Meade in his new role as commanding-general, were the ones that offered no objections to his plans during the battle of Gettysburg yet turned out to be the greatest critics of his decisions.] Unfamiliarity also did not lend itself to unit cohesiveness. There was no substitute for the rapport built from interactions, struggles, deprivations, and achievements experienced as a team. Professionalism alone did not insure cooperation.[24]

Familiarity, at least, increased the chances that officers were more likely to bend or break the rules and circumvent the chain of command to address an emergency situation. On July 2nd, for example, Col. Patrick O'Rorke's 140th New York Infantry broke the chain of command by ignoring his existing order to move forward to help Gen. Sickles and, instead, assisted Gen. Gouverneur Warren, Chief of Engineers, by diverting his regiment to Little Round Top. The chief reason for O'Rorke's cooperation was due to familiarity. Warren was his former brigade commander. Had O'Rorke not recognized Warren, perhaps he would not have risked a court martial by ignoring the standing order of his brigade. As a result, O'Rorke's decision to divert his regiment was instrumental in securing the hill.

As previously mentioned, Lee possessed the invaluable benefit of familiarity in the role of commanding-general over the newly appointed Meade. Lee held the position for over a year and officers in the Army of Northern Virginia were well acquainted with their leader. Officers in the Army of the Potomac, on the other hand, were subjected to a succession of commanding-generals that seemed never-ending. Each commander imprinted his style and each battle lost brought forth another commanding-general. Meade was the seventh in a little more than two years.

When the Army of the Potomac and the Army of Northern Virginia struck their tents to start the Gettysburg campaign, no one could anticipate the magnitude of change that would befall the leadership in the upcoming operation. Besides the recently reorganized Army of Northern Virginia, revisions in leadership for the Army of the Potomac would be just as dramatic as the campaign progressed. As mentioned earlier, the Army of the Potomac added units from other military departments and state militias prepared to assist with the emergency. In the process, new chains of command were created with new leaders and unfamiliar relationships.

As new chains of command were formed, relationships between former commander and subordinate dissolved along with leadership style, continuity, and familiarity. At Gettysburg, the Lee/Longstreet/Jackson team was gone, along with the rapport that existed with it. Now it was the Lee/Longstreet/Ewell/Hill team.

Gettysburg was the first battle to test these new relationships. If Lee continued to operate and issue orders in the same style as he did with the old group, it could be viewed as a subtle expression of confidence that his new team possessed the intuitive skills necessary to interact like the old group. However, to presume that all would react to "reading" their commander's customary broad instructions with the intuitive ability of the old group, would have risky consequences for an untested team in its first battle. The new corps commanders surely needed the supervision of the commanding-general, through his staff, to insure they understood their new roles and that they would be instructed with enough information to achieve their assignments.

Command Changes: The Domino Effect

The majority of command changes in the Gettysburg campaign was from combat casualties and at all ranks. High rank was not associated with safer duty. Unlike today's wars where high-ranking officers are more insulated and distant from danger, Civil War generals were in the midst of the fray, often up front inspiring their men, often mounted, and often prime targets for marksmen.

Frequent exposure to danger and resultant casualties of generals created openings at the top, which, in turn, triggered a domino effect down the chain of command. While Gen. Hooker's departure was by resignation, consider the cascade effect caused at the commanding-general's level:

1. On June 28th, 1863, Gen. Hooker was replaced by the 5th Corps commander, Gen. Meade.
2. Meade's corps command was filled by the 5th Corps' division commander, Gen. Sykes.
3. Sykes' division command was filled by brigade commander, Gen. Ayres.
4. Ayres' brigade command was filled by regimental commander, Col. Day.
5. Day's regimental command [at Gettysburg with 5 companies] was filled by Capt. Levi C. Bootes.
6. And so on down the line within the regiment from Lt. Col., Major, Captain, and 1st Lt.

Besides the ripple effect from any type of changes in the high command, battles casualties suddenly caused hundreds of revisions across the army. During the first day's battle at Gettysburg, for example, Gen. Gabriel Paul, Union brigade commander, suffered a severe wound during the defense of Oak Ridge. The brigade command transferred to Col. Samuel Leonard, 13th Mass. After Leonard was wounded, the command transferred to Col. Adrian Root, 94th N. Y. After Root was wounded, the command transferred to Col. Richard Coulter, 11th Pa. Under heavy fire during the July 3rd cannonade, Col. Coulter, then on Cemetery Hill, was wounded and temporarily disabled. The command was transferred to Col. Peter Lyle, 90th Pa., but soon after, Col. Coulter recovered enough and resumed command of the brigade. [25]

ARMY OF THE POTOMAC'S HIGH COMMAND

Maj. Gen. George Meade
Commanding General

Maj. Gen. Alfred Pleasonton
Cavalry Corps

Brig. Gen. Henry Hunt
Chief of Artillery

Maj. Gen. John Reynolds
1st Corps

Maj. Gen. Winfield Hancock
2nd Corps

Maj. Gen. Daniel Sickles
3rd Corps

Maj. Gen. George Sykes
5th Corps

Maj. Gen. John Sedgwick
6th Corps

Maj. Gen. O.O. Howard
11th Corps

Maj. Gen. Henry Slocum
12th Corps

Army of Northern Virginia's High Command

Gen. Robert E. Lee
Commanding General

Maj. Gen. Jeb Stuart
Cavalry Commander

Brig. Gen. Wm. Pendleton
Chief of Artillery

Lt. Gen.
James Longstreet
1st Corps

Lt. Gen.
Richard Ewell
2nd Corps

Lt. Gen
A. P. Hill
3rd Corps

In another example, on July 2nd, the 11th N. J. Infantry regiment, 3rd Corps, had its leadership decimated while fighting near the Klingel farm along the Emmitsburg road. In this action, the regiment's commander, Col. R. McAllister, fell severely wounded by a Minie ball in his left leg and a piece of shell in his right foot. Major Philip J. Kearny, the next most senior officer present, was struck by a Minie ball in the knee. Both McAllister and Kearny were carried to the rear. Capt. Luther Martin, the senior officer present, then took over command. Soon Capt. Martin along with Capt. Doraster Logan were wounded and killed while being taken to the rear. A moment later, Captain Andrew Ackerman fell dead and Capt. William Lloyd was wounded. Lt. John Schoonover, the senior officer present, assumed and remained in command despite being twice wounded. [26]

At Gettysburg, the Official Records for the Army of the Potomac's Order of Battle listed 170 command changes; the Official Records for the Army of Northern Virginia's Order of Battle listed 101 command changes. These figures do not include Meade's promotion, the restructuring of Lee's army near the beginning of the campaign, the temporary appointments to wing commanders, or promotions triggered within regiments below the command level.

Level of Change	Army of the Potomac	Army of Northern Virginia
Corps	4	0
Division	6	5
Brigade	25	19
Regiment	118	71
Artillery Reserve	1	0
Artillery Brig./Btn	1	1
Batteries	15	5
Total	170	101 [27]

Command Changes in Supporting Roles

In addition, any units used as a reserve in combat were subject to being broken apart piecemeal with scattered commands sent to support anyplace on the field where needed. In the process, fragmented commands lost its leadership. On July 2nd, for example, Union Col. George Burling, 3rd Corps, had his infantry brigade temporarily disassembled into regiments and singly disbursed to support others needing emergency assistance. This dismantled force resulted in a brigadeless commander and his staff that were relegated to mere spectators. "My command" Burling wrote, "now all being taken from me and separated, no two regiments being together, and being under the command of the different brigade commanders to whom they had reported, I, with my staff, reported to General Humphreys for instructions, remaining with him for some time." Maj. Gen. John Sedgwick also suffered a similar plight when his Union 6th Corps arrived onto the field and was parceled out for use at different points. [28]

Frictions with: Senior Commander on the Field/Wing Commands/Corps commands

The title *senior commander on the field* needs no explanation other than to say that it transferred the command responsibility to the senior-most officer present. If another more senior officer arrived, he took command. This transfer of command and corresponding responsibility was traditionally done by seniority protocol but it disregarded the fact that new, more senior arrivals knew the least about what had already happened, what was then happening, and what was about to happen. When Union Gen. Henry Slocum arrived at Gettysburg on July 1st, for example, he was the senior commander on the field but was uninterested and ill prepared in taking over a situation he knew little or nothing about.

Wing Commands

On the roads to Gettysburg, seven Union infantry corps were scattered over hundreds of square miles. In the absence of the commanding-general it was essential to have a coordinator for units too distant for army headquarters to control. To do this, the Army of the Potomac used wing commanders. Wing commands were to be used as a command of maneuver, to coordinate cooperation within a wing, or with another wing. Wing commanders were senior corps commanders assigned temporary control over two or more other corps.

The domino effect in the use of wing commands was almost as dramatic as the change in commanding-general mentioned above. When Gen. John Reynolds was acting as wing commander, for example, Gen. Abner Doubleday's role was upgraded from senior division commander to 1st Corps commander, the senior brigade commander was bumped up to division command, the senior regimental commander was bumped up to brigade command, and so on within the regiment down to the company level.

The responsibility of wing commanders varied according to the wishes of the commanding-general. The assignment of wing commands could be modified with two options: 1. A corps commander controlled multiple corps and was temporarily detached from his normal corps command. 2. A corps commander controlled multiple corps without relinquishing control of his normal corps command.

Just before Gettysburg, on June 30, option one was used. In the absence of Gen. Meade, Gen. Reynolds was assigned to command the right wing of the Union army [which later became the left wing at Gettysburg.] The wing included the 1st, 3rd, and 11th Corps. Reynolds ordinarily commanded the 1st Corps but he relinquished this command to Gen. Doubleday. On July 2nd, Gen. Slocum was temporarily assigned to command the right wing which included the 5th, 6th, and 12th Corps. He acted in this capacity from July 1st to July 5th. Ordinarily he commanded the 12th Corps but he relinquished this command to Gen. Alpheus Williams.

Just after the battle, on July 5th, wing commands were assigned as in option two. Meade ordered that "General [John] Sedgwick will, without relinquishing command of his corps, assume command and direct the movement of the corps forming the right—First, Sixth, and Third. General Slocum will, without relinquishing command of his corps forming the left—Twelfth and Second. General [Oliver] Howard, without relinquishing the command of his corps, assume command and direct the movements of the corps forming the center—Fifth and Eleventh." Perhaps option two was chosen here because of command frictions created with option one [discussed later] during the battle of Gettysburg. [29]

Corps Commands

At Gettysburg, the Army of Northern Virginia had three large infantry corps numbering about 21,000 men each. The Army of the Potomac had seven smaller infantry corps averaging about 12,000 men each. Having larger corps, but fewer of them, had benefits: it reduced bureaucracy and staff requirements in the organization; it simplified the chain of command by needing fewer avenues of communication; it permitted faster decision-making, unfettered by multiple opinions and disagreements. The larger Confederate infantry corps also protected more ground than their enemy counterparts. This feature lent itself to handling situations within their own spheres of operation by supplying support controlled by the same corps commander and, therefore, lessened the need for outside help. Conversely, fewer commanders meant less talent to draw from and less experience to help in planning; fewer staffs were not able to deal with as many details as the staffs of their enemy counterparts.

The Army of the Potomac, having smaller corps and more of them, had benefits as well: smaller corps increased mobility. It was easier to assemble or move a smaller, self-contained infantry corps without separating its command [beneficial in the campaign but not too beneficial at Gettysburg]. More corps provided flexibility in performing a greater number of missions. Conversely, smaller corps protected less ground, the need for help beyond the corps command was greater and complicated matters when units crossed other spheres of command. With smaller corps, Meade had to deal with seven commanders, either indirectly through headquarters staff or through personal visits on the field, interviews at headquarters, or in a group council. By having a greater number of corps commanders, consensus was more difficult to achieve [Differing opinions in councils were evident from votes taken.]. Consensus, however, was not as important as having more relevant ideas presented in discussions to help the commanding-general plan his next moves.

The roles of senior commander on the field, wing commander, and corps commander seemed to blend into indistinguishable roles and cause serious command frictions for the Army of the Potomac at Gettysburg. Command changes which created the frictions were caused by death or injury, arrivals of senior officers, and deviating from seniority protocol. The revisions in the Army of the Potomac's high command were significant. The following is just a sample of one day's activity, July 1st, and reflects the fluid nature of an army concentrating during a battle:

1. The battle began with Gen. John Buford, cavalry division commander, acting as *senior commander on the field*.
2. Gen. John Reynolds, *left wing commander*, arrived, took over as *senior commander on the field*, and killed shortly thereafter.

3. After Reynolds' death, Gen. Abner Doubleday, then acting as 1st Corps commander, took over [briefly] and issued orders as *senior commander on the field.* [30]
4. Gen. Oliver Howard, 11th corps commander, arrived and after hearing of Reynolds' death, took over and issued orders as *senior commander on the field.*
5. Gen. Winfield Hancock, 2nd Corps commander, arrived. Although junior to Howard, but by order of Gen. Meade, Hancock took over as *senior commander on the field.*
6. Gen. Henry Slocum, 12th Corps commander, arrived and took over as *senior commander on the field* after Hancock departed.
7. Gen. Meade arrived around midnight and took over as commanding-general.

Some additional confusion as to who was in command on July 1st was attributed to Gen. Thomas Rowley. He was promoted from his 1st Corps brigade command to acting commander of Gen. Doubleday's division. At one point, after Gen. Reynolds' death and for some unknown reason, Rowley thought he was the 1st Corps commander. He rode about giving orders to troops, some say were unintelligible. Col. Charles Wainright and others thought he was drunk. When he withdrew towards Gettysburg, he fell off his horse and had to be helped out of a ditch. Later that day he was arrested and removed from the battlefield under guard. [His next duty assignment was a draft office in Maine.] [31]

Without notification, subordinate commanders could not keep pace with command changes and, consequently, the chain of command blurred. During the time of the change from Howard to Hancock on July 1st, Gen. Meade, at Taneytown, Md., received a copy of a message from Gen. Howard, as senior commander, [written before Hancock's takeover] to Gen. Sickles, in Emmitsburg, Md., which ordered the 3rd Corps to Gettysburg. Since Meade had placed Hancock in command over Howard, Meade sent off a dispatch to Sickles canceling Howard's directive and "to hold on until you hear from General Hancock." [Meade was concerned about leaving the approaches to Emmitsburg unguarded.] Before Sickles received Meade's dispatch "to hold" he was already moving forward to help Howard, the perceived commander on the field at Gettysburg. At the same time, Sickles, using his own judgment, kept two brigades and two batteries back, "assuming that the approaches through Emmitsburg toward our left and rear must not be uncovered."

Sickles then received Meade's announcement that Hancock was in command at Gettysburg. The confusion as to who was in charge is evident in Sickles' reply to Meade's directive:

> General Hancock is not in command--General Howard commands...Nothing less than the earnest and frequent appeals of General Howard, and his supposed danger, could have induced me to move from the position assigned to me in general orders; but I believed the emergency justified my movement. Shall I return to my position at Emmitsburg, or shall I remain and report to Howard? [32]

Sickles, despite his later controversy on July 2nd, must be complimented in the way he handled this conflict of orders. Sickles' intuitive reasoning and his action, eventually approved by Meade, helped limit the confusion as to who was in charge.

Compare the two generals' [Sickles and Slocum] decisions regarding Howard's desperate pleas for help as the battle of Gettyburg opened. Lt. Col. Thomas Rafferty, 71st N.Y., 3rd Corps, described the situation:

> Here was a dilemma that might have perplexed a weaker man. In fact, another of our corps commanders [Slocum], and one of the best of them too, on receiving the same despatch [as Sickles], refused to move his corps without an order from General Meade. However, it did not trouble Sickles long. He obeyed the dictates of common sense and at once hurried his corps forward to place it where it would do the most good. [33]

Unexpectedly breaking the seniority protocol, as with Hancock's temporary assignment on July 1st, did not promote cooperation during the crucial moments following the Union retreat through Gettysburg and subsequent efforts in rallying the troops to defend Cemetery Hill. A bewildered Howard wrote: "General Hancock came to me about this time and said General Meade had sent him on hearing the state of affairs; that he had given him his instructions while under the impression that he was my senior. We agreed at once that that was no time for talking, and that General Hancock should further arrange the troops, and placed the batteries upon the left of the Baltimore Pike, while I should take the right of the same." [34]

Subsequently, Gen. Hancock rode up to Gen. Doubleday, 1st Corps commander, and informed him that he was now in command. Doubleday said, "[Hancock] directed me to send a force to support a battery, which had been established on the lower range of hills...I complied...Immediately afterward orders came from Major-General Howard, who ranked Hancock, to send the troops in another direction. This occasioned at the time some little delay and confusion." [35]

Howard said that he neither recognized Hancock's assignment as his superior on July 1st nor did he state that he relinquished command to him. Howard said, "About 7 p.m. Generals Slocum and Sickles arrived at the cemetery. A formal order was at the same time put into my hands, placing General Hancock in command of the left wing. But General Slocum being present, and senior, I turned the command over to him, and resumed the direct command of the Eleventh Corps; whereupon General Hancock repaired to the headquarters of General Meade." It must have riled Howard not just to be replaced by an officer who was his junior, but one that had freshly arrived, was ignorant of circumstances, and placed in charge over a commander who had spent most of the day thickly involved in the fighting. Slocum, incidentally, accepted Hancock's overall command assignment until Hancock departed to see Meade at Taneytown Md. [36]

Arrival of Lesser Commands

In addition, as the armies concentrated around Gettysburg, scattered corps, divisions, and brigades arrived on the battlefield piecemeal. Some were without their commanders. In the absence of a corps commander, the senior-most division commander was in charge, in the absence of the division commander, the senior-most brigade commander was in charge, in the absence of the brigade commander, the senior-most regimental commander was in charge. On July 1st, for example, Gen. Joseph Carr, 3rd Corps brigade commander, in the absence of his division commander and his corps commander, acted on their behalf by ordering the division to Gettysburg "for the purpose of selecting a position for the corps…"

Until the armies had finally concentrated and all commanders were present, the protocol of seniority called for continuously shifting command responsibility to the unit's senior-most officer present. [37]

Lack of Notification

Command changes required notification to appropriate personnel. Notification was a crucial step in preserving who had the responsibility of the operation and the authority to issue orders. Announcing command changes, however, was difficult to accomplish in battle. Commands were broken apart, temporarily re-assigned to other commands during urgent circumstances, or shuffled about to different parts of the field. Combat conditions slowed down or stopped communication altogether.

Lack of notification could convert a coordinated attack into a series of independent assaults where smaller units operated on their own hook. For example, on July 2nd, minutes into the Confederate attack against the Union left flank, division commander, Gen. John Hood, was taken out of action with a severe wound. His predetermined replacement was Gen. Evander Law who, at the moment, was leading his Alabama brigade into battle on the far right of the division. Law, uninformed of Hood's wounding, continued leading his men at the brigade level during this entire action. It is unclear when Law assumed command of the division and the existing information on this suggests that Law's guidance at the division level played no important role in the outcome of this action. The division, in effect then, was going into battle as four independent brigades, absent of coordination, and short on leadership at the division level. [38]

Lack of notification caused misunderstandings and disputes over control of forces or sectors of ground. In using wing commands, for example, there seemed to be no clear understanding when the wing command assignment terminated. Apparently, termination was an understanding by assumption rather than a formal method of notification.

On July 2nd, for example, Gen. Meade assigned Gen. Slocum as the right wing commander. Gen. Williams, division commander, replaced Slocum as 12th Corps commander. Meade, in his after action report, failed to recognize Williams' contribution as a corps commander. He later regretted the omission but also stated he "did not expect or design him to be so." Furthermore, Meade, at his late night war council, on July 2nd, with headquarters staff and corps commanders, said he was "puzzled to account for [Williams'] presence" since Slocum was also there... Meade stated, "I cannot say anything more beyond the fact that General Williams' commanding the corps was not impressed on my mind..." [39]

Meade told Slocum that at one point he assigned him [Slocum] to prepare an attack on July 2nd, using the 5th, 6th, and 12th Corps, "but inasmuch as both these corps were removed to another part of the field early in the afternoon, and never returned, I presumed you would understand your command over them was only temporary, and ceased with their removal."

Meade's comment is noteworthy when reviewing the events surrounding the senior command changes on July 1st. In brief, using replacement by seniority, Gen. Howard took over as senior commander after the death of Gen. Reynolds and, at the end of the day, Gen. Slocum took over as senior commander. Meade did not issue an order to cause these changes. He simply expected the senior-most commander on the field to take charge. But in between these two command changes, Meade broke the seniority protocol by placing Hancock in charge. In this instance, Meade undoubtedly, caused some of the confusion by changing the customary seniority protocol but, at the same time, assumed that Slocum, as a wing commander, should have known when to stop this assignment and go back to commanding the 12th Corps.

So from Meade's point of view, on July 2nd, he was initially issuing orders to Slocum as a wing commander, then later that day, as a corps commander. From Slocum's viewpoint he was receiving orders as a wing commander for the remainder of the battle but never as a corps commander. Consequently, Williams was out of the communications loop as acting corps commander from Meade's perspective despite the fact that Slocum had relinquished control of the 12th Corps to him.

This confusion of control had the potential to cause severe problems had Williams not received direction from Slocum in his capacity as "wing commander." The effects of this misunderstanding, if any, can only be surmised, but the fact remains that three important commanders, Meade, Slocum, and Williams, were operating with misunderstood responsibilities and issuing or receiving orders in a mistaken capacity and affecting thousands of troops. [40]

Much of the above confusion in the Army of the Potomac could have been avoided by the ordinary performance of Meade's staff. Keeping commanders current on the status of their command assignment was not a superior feat in the course of a staff function – it was a requirement. Army headquarters was the place to determine when to revoke the assignment of a command. If there was an atmosphere of doubt about this procedure, and there certainly was, attentiveness to handling such a problem was of the utmost importance, especially since it affected such high levels of command. It is obvious that a formal method of notification was needed to terminate temporary assignments rather than relying on any subordinate commander to somehow discern when it was time to conclude them.

In the time frame of the Gettysburg campaign, consider the changes in the Army of the Potomac's high command. It experienced an exceptional high rate of turnover in leadership at the corps level and above.

Level of Command

1. **Commanding-general**

   Meade replaced Hooker.

2. **Senior commander on the field**:
   - A. Buford started the battle as senior commander on the field.
   - B. Reynolds took over and was killed.
   - C. Replaced by Doubleday.
   - D. Replaced by Howard.
   - E. Hancock arrived to take command.
   - F. Hancock left and Slocum took over.
   - G. Meade arrived.

3. **Corps Commands:**
   - A. **1st Corps**:
     1. Doubleday replaced Reynolds after he was killed.
     2. Newton replaced Doubleday.
   - B. **2nd Corps**:
     1. Gibbon replaced Hancock when he took over as senior commander on the field on July 1st.
     2. Hancock returned to corps command.
     3. Hancock injured on July 3rd.
     4. Gibbon again replaced Hancock.
     5. William Hays replaced Gibbon.
   - C. **3rd Corps**
     1. Sickles injured on July 2nd.
     2. Birney replaced Sickles.
     3. Hancock temporarily replaced Birney.
     4. Birney replaced Hancock.

5. French replaced Birney

D. **5th Corps**

1. Sykes remained as commander but his forces were parceled out to support other troops.

E. **6th Corps**

1. Sedgwick remained as commander but his forces were parceled out to support other troops.

F. **11th Corps**

1. On July 1st, Howard replaced Reynolds as senior commander on the field.
2. Schurz replaced Howard.
3. Howard reverted back to corps command

G. **12th Corps**

1. On July 1st, Slocum took over as senior commander on the field, then as wing commander on July 2nd.
2. Williams replaced Slocum.

Turmoil from changes in the high command for the Army of the Potomac is quite remarkable. It is not difficult to imagine how the rash of changes bred confusion as to who was in control at any one time during the battle. Comparatively, the Army of Northern Virginia had significantly fewer changes in the high commands: the commanding-general remained the same; at the beginning of the battle, Gen. A. P. Hill's 3rd Corps division commander, Gen. Henry Heth, acted as senior commander on the field followed by the orderly progression of command changes from senior generals' arrivals, including Gen. Lee; there were no disruptions at the corps command level. All three Confederate infantry corps commanders remained in their leadership positions throughout the battle. None were injured [Gen. Ewell was shot in his wooden leg.].

Command Summary

Both armies suffered from command frictions in the Gettysburg campaign. It is conclusive, however, that the Army of the Potomac suffered this condition far more than the Army of Northern Virginia. It did so for several reasons:

1. Mixing forces from different commands on the same ground caused confusion in the chain of command:

   A. On a strategic level, the Army of the Potomac moved across military departments outside its traditional area of operations. The Army of Northern Virginia did not experience this problem since they were in Union territory.

   B. On a tactical level, the Union army was on the defensive and moved troops to meet threats. Every infantry corps, or major parts of every corps present, moved from ground outside its originally assigned area. In comparison, the Army of Northern Virginia moved far fewer units into operating areas assigned to other corps.

2. The number of command changes from the division level and above, including the Army of the Potomac's commanding-general, was more than double that of the Army of Northern Virginia. Every Union infantry corps commander at the battle of Gettysburg was either replaced, lost through death or injury, elevated to a higher command, or the corps commanders' role was degraded when many of their units were assigned to support forces outside the corps. High level changes triggered a domino effect and multiplied modifications in command positions to the lowest levels.

3. Changes broke continuity of command, changed style of operation, introduced officers to unaccustomed assignments, and new roles needed a period of adjustment.

4. The use of wing commanders by the Army of the Potomac was a useful tool in maneuvering units but needed formal notification when the assignment would cease.

5. Compared to Meade, the value of Lee's established relationship with his army and the continuity of command which Lee brought to Gettysburg cannot be underestimated. Lee's charismatic character energized the Army of Northern Virginia to perform almost superhuman feats of endurance and self-sacrifice with little complaint. Lee's extended term as commanding-general preserved continuity of command as it entered the Gettysburg

campaign. Lee's style of command with his new team of corps commanders, however, should have been altered to reduce the chance of command frictions by providing more supervision in the first battle following the army's reorganization.

Meade, on the other hand, entered the battle of Gettysburg with few or no advantages similar to what Lee possessed in the role of commanding-general. He was new to the position. Continuity of command was broken when Gen. Hooker departed; it changed the style of command, relationships, and familiarity within the Army of the Potomac. And although Meade was the commanding-general, for all intent and purpose it was still Hooker's army, unreflective of Meade's standards of performance. Defending home ground, however, forged a determination in the Army of the Potomac to help overcome such shortcomings. [41]

Part 2: Communication Frictions

> Many...defining moments (that make all the difference) come from 'crucial' or 'breakthrough' conversations with important people in emotionally charged situations where the decisions made take us down one of several roads, each of which leads to an entirely different destination. [42]

Protocol

Communication is a transfer of information and meaning, a three-step process of composing, transferring, and receiving. Communication frictions in the Gettysburg campaign occurred at every stage of this process. Major operations were bungled from messages composed with conflicting instructions, vague directions, or dual meanings. Communications contained insufficient guidance or clarity in purpose. Some messages were corrupted in transmission, obsolete before delivery, or misunderstood by recipients. There were also problems from disregarded communication protocol used in the chain of command.

The chain of command defined the hierarchy of leadership and the flow of responsibility in following orders. It was a guideline which prescribed strict paths of communication within the organization. Protocol maintained order over chaos. It channeled information through all intermediate levels in the chain of command between the sender and receiver; it allowed subordinates to receive instructions from their immediate superiors; it prevented the issuance of conflicting orders from more than one superior.

A commanding-general, for example, wishing to communicate to a specific regiment, sent the message to the unit's corps command, which sent it to the division, then to the brigade, and finally the regiment. Adherence to the rules avoided skipping anyone in the sequence, and it avoided the appearance that a subordinate commander was communicating to others and bypassing his immediate superior.

Following communication protocol, however, added some problems. It slowed down the transmission of information by passing through more points of transfer. This included messages where delivery time was critical. More points of transfer also increased the chance of written messages getting misplaced or verbal messages getting corrupted from the faulty memories of messengers while en route.

In battle, paths of communication often skipped middle layers in the chain of command. Expediency sent staff officers directly to lower commands to launch actions or make on-the-spot decisions as representatives of their commander. Bypassed commanders sometimes felt personally slighted because it diminished their importance in the eyes of their subordinates. While ignoring protocol may have ruffled some commanders left out of the message sequence, the perceived slight was, more often than not, sorted out amicably afterwards.

Circumventing the chain of command, however, not only left commanders out of the communication loop, but it also removed their responsibility in the outcome of an action in which their units participated and where they had no opportunity to command. Bypassing also sidestepped the chain of communication which, in turn, affected the bypassed commander's coordination of his command and placed subordinate commanders in the position of accepting orders from superiors or a superiors' staff to whom they did not report. In May, 1863 Gen. A. P. Hill, 3rd Corps commander, Army of Northern Virginia, complained about Lee's headquarters staff bypassing him to communicate to his subordinates. Gen. Lee responded:

> My opinion is, that my chiefs of staff, in executing general orders in relation to this army, can properly give directions to their subordinates in each corps relating to their several departments without my sending the order directly to the corps commander, and so down. It is the duty of the corps staff officers, on receiving these directions, to apprise the corps commander; so of the division staff officers.
>
> If any objection to their execution exists, the commanders should apprise their principals, and, if necessary, suspend the execution till sustained. Otherwise I shall have to give all directions, and the corps and division commanders, &c., have to attend to all the staff operations of their commands in addition to their military operations, which, in the field, in time of action, &c., may be the cause of delay and loss, and at least half of the advantages of the general staff impaired....
>
> I request, therefore, that all orders from the chiefs of staff departments may be considered as emanating directly from me, and executed accordingly. [43]

There was a proper etiquette for bypassing the chain of command. Deviating from the rules, however, was not taken lightly. Efforts to insure proper etiquette in breaking protocol sometimes went to great lengths to make the transaction official. For example, on July 2nd, Gen. Crawford moved his Federal division, 5th Corps, along Blacksmith Shop Road in the rear of Little Round Top and towards the battle. Already under orders to one destination, he was interrupted with a plea for help elsewhere. Crawford wrote:

> An officer arrived, very much excited; pointed over in the direction of some hills, which were directly in my front, and said that the enemy were attacking those hills; that it was most important to hold them and that the troops there were in need of assistance. I asked him who he was. He said he was Captain Moore, of General Meade's staff. I said to him, "very well, that is sufficient authority for me. If you give me General Meade's order I will go at once, if you will show me the direction. I am expecting an officer from General [George] Sykes' staff, who commands the corps." He [Capt. Moore] said, " I cannot give you General Meade's order." I said, "there are some general officers to my right. General Slocum is there, commanding the Twelfth Corps. Bring me his order, and I will go."
>
> He galloped down the road, and in a few minutes returned with the order from General Slocum. I moved the column rapidly with him and arrived in a few moments on the field. [44]

In another example on July 2nd the Confederates had assaulted and pushed Gen. Sickles' Union line back from his forward position on the Emmitsburg road, overrunning and capturing Watson's artillery pieces. Lt. Samuel Peeples, an officer in Watson's battery, sought the help of any infantry soldiers that could help recapture the lost guns. Peeples caught the attention of Capt. Fasset, aide to Gen. David Birney, division commander, Sickles' 3rd Corps, and explained his need for troops to retake the guns. Fasset soon came into contact with Maj. Hugo Hildebrandt, 39th N. Y. Infantry, 2nd Corps, and ordered him to retake the guns in the name of Gen. Birney. Hildebrandt, however, was from Hays' division and declined to respond since he was not in Birney's command. Fasset then asked Hildebrandt to which command he belonged. Hildebrandt answered Hancock's. Fasset simply reworded his order to retake the guns by order of Gen. Hancock. This restatement of an order was enough to satisfy Hildebrandt who then ordered his regiment into action and recovered the guns. [Thirty years later, Fasset received the Medal of Honor for his participation in this action.] [45]

In still another example, Union Gen. Samuel Zook, brigade commander, Caldwell's division, experienced a similar plight. On July 2nd, Sickles' 3rd Corps and two brigades from the 5th Corps were about to lose control of the Wheatfield and its surrounding ground. Zook's brigade, following the rear of his division, was already en route to help. Soon after the march began, Maj. Henry Tremain, senior aide-de-camp to Sickles, was sent by Gen. Sickles to lead Caldwell's division into the fray. By happenstance Tremain came into contact with the rear of Caldwell's moving column and bumped into Zook. Tremain and Zook were strangers to each other. By now Tremain realized that Caldwell's column was misdirected. It was heading towards Little Round Top and away from the Wheatfield.

In following protocol, Tremain said he "...adhered to all the formalities and inquired where his division general could be found, at the same time explaining the urgency..." Because of the critical situation, Zook was then asked to detach the brigade from his division and move immediately to the Wheatfield. In replying to this plea for help from an unfamiliar officer, Zook explained that the orders were to follow his division. Tremain repeated his request along with a promise to provide a proper order from Gen. Sickles, which would absolve Zook of any perceived breach in the chain of command protocol. Zook acquiesced to Tremain's plea for help but only after he made Tremain verbalize the request to validate it. "Sir," Zook said, "if you will give me the order of General Sickles I will obey it." To which Tremain replied, "General Sickles' order, general, is that you file your brigade to the right and move into action here." [Accounts vary as to who the aide was that diverted Zook. Tremain later said he was not the aide Zook spoke to but that he conducted Zook's brigade to the action.]

These examples reflect the discipline shown during the turmoil of battle, the respect given for the proper protocol in the chain of command, and that deviating from standing orders was a serious issue. Zook's choice to break away from his division and re-direct his brigade resulted in his timely arrival at the Wheatfield and is commendable [Zook was, unfortunately, killed in this action.]. There was a side issue to Zook's action which created another communication friction. Zook was detached from his division without Caldwell's knowledge or consent. It is unclear at what point Caldwell noticed that one of his brigades was missing. [46]

The provision, allowing deviation of protocol, worked. It addressed an emergency situation and transferred responsibility to the proper command level. At first glance, Crawford's, Hildebrandt's and Zook's attention to protocol seems too meticulous at such an intense moment. But without a sense of order prevailing over the excitement of battle, it is easy to see how events such as these could and did destroy the chain of command and sever leaders' connections with their own forces. Undoubtedly the outcome of the action would have been greatly altered had these three officers insisted on strict protocol and refused assistance during those critical moments.

While communication protocol in the chain of command defined the flow of responsibility, the procedure was more complex than senior officers simply giving orders to any subordinates. Rank alone was not enough to circumvent the chain of command. A general from a given unit, for example, could not freely move about the battlefield giving orders to subordinates of other units. Likewise, subordinate officers did not readily follow orders from superiors outside their chain of command. Breaking protocol depended on circumstances. Subjectivity was frequently used to determine if the action was proper and this led to communication frictions.

Col. Freeman McGilvery, commanding a Union brigade of reserve artillery, gives us an example during the cannonade on July 3rd. McGilvery was under orders from the Chief of Artillery, Gen. Henry Hunt to hold his fire. McGilvery said: "[Enemy] fire was very rapid and inaccurate, most of the projectiles passing from 20 to 100 feet over our lines. About one-half hour after the commencement, some General [Hancock] commanding the infantry line ordered three of the batteries to return the fire. After the discharge of a few rounds, I ordered the fire to cease and the men to be covered." [47]

General Hunt, Chief of Artillery, for the Army of the Potomac, referred to this incident later: "One of the corps or division commanders, Hancock I think, nearly ruined himself by insisting that the batteries along his line should keep up a heavy fire, after...[Hunt], had ordered them to cease. The consequence was they expended all their ammunition, and had none when the tug came. Fortunately Colonel McGilvery, an old Maine sea captain, had command of four or five batteries from the reserve on his right [Hancock's left], and refused point blank to obey. I say fortunately, for when the enemy got close up, McGilvery having all fresh and ready [sic], poured in the ugliest kind of oblique fire on him."

At the same time, Capt. John Hazard, commanding the 2nd Corps artillery brigade in the Union center, was placed in the same predicament as McGilvery. Hunt told him to hold his fire, but Hazard was under the direct control of Hancock and could not refuse his demands to open fire. [48]

Without judging the correctness of which order was best, the point to be made here is that two superiors were giving conflicting orders to a subordinate. Ordinarily Hunt had direct control over the artillery reserve, which included McGilvery. But the standing rule was that the duties of the Chief of Artillery were "exclusively administrative", "unless specially ordered by the commanding-general," while the battle line was controlled by the infantry commander. In the above example, Hancock controlled the battlefront where McGilvery's guns were located. [49]

The Hunt/Hancock dispute originated on July 2nd when General Slocum approached Meade to report a gap between his 12th Corps' troops and Cemetery Hill. Meade told Hunt (as nearly as Hunt could recollect): "This is your affair. Take the proper measures to provide against the attack, and make the line safe with artillery until it is properly occupied." Perhaps Meade should have explained the time limit, if any, to Hunt's assignment or Hunt should have asked. Hunt concluded: "This, with his previous instructions, left me no room to doubt his intent as to my duties and powers, and it was under a full sense of the responsibility thus imposed that I immediately assumed the active command of the Artillery and exercised it during the remainder of the battle." [50]

Unfortunately subordinate commanders were placed at the center of a dispute between two squabbling generals. Hancock complained of the "Artillery Captain" [who] refused to obey his order to open fire. Hunt argued back: "[Hancock] charges me with obstructing his operations at the Battle of Gettysburg, to such an extent as to compel him to 'threaten force' on his own line, in order to make a battery fire on the enemy." [51]

As for the "Artillery Captain", Hunt said:

> He had better bring him to trial then, if a General can't command the troops under his orders I can't help him." "But," said Meade, "if the Captain was not a part of his command." "Then," I replied, "It depends on circumstances if the Captain should obey him." Oh! said Meade "a battery Captain must obey a General who gives him an order." I said "the same principles of military command apply to the artillery as to other

troops. A general has no more right to order about the batteries of another corp. or division than his own then he has to order about their infantry or cavalry regiment. Let any General undertake to give orders to my battery in violation of my orders, and I will soon teach the Captain who obeys him unless the facts warrant the different action, whether he can obey. If he must obey any casual General who may come along & fancy to give him orders he must by the same rules obey any Colonel, Major or Captain of higher rank who chooses to commence to control him. He will obey at his own peril. [52]

Staff communication

The communications center of an army was, of course, its headquarters. It was equipped with all the hardware necessary for communications such as signal flags, visual aids such as binoculars, and supplies such as journals, reference books, records, and maps. The command center was surrounded with staff officers skilled in specific disciplines, aides to carry out the wishes of its leader, and guards to provide security and protection for headquarters personnel. An army headquarters was not a tent but more like a tent city fully involved with the activity of many, scurrying about performing their duties. The complement of men assigned to Meade's headquarters during the battle of Gettysburg, for example, numbered 3,486. [53]

The top headquarters staff for both armies at Gettysburg:

Army of the Potomac

Chief-of-Staff Maj. Gen. Daniel Butterfield
Provost-Marshall-General Brig. Gen. Marsena Patrick
Adj. Gen. Brig. Gen. Seth Williams
Inspector Gen. Brig. Gen. Edmund Schriver
Q/M Gen. Brig. Gen. Rufus Ingalls
Chief of Commissary of Subsistence Col. Henry F. Clarke
Surgeon, Chief of Medical Dept. Maj. Jonathan Lettermen
Chief of Cavalry Maj. Gen. Alfred Pleasonton
Chief of Artillery Brig. Gen. Henry Hunt
Chief Signal Officer Capt. L. B. Norton

Army of the Potomac's headquarters camp, Brandy Station, Virginia

Army of Northern Virginia

Adj. Gen. Col. W.H. Taylor
Aide-de-Camp Col. C.S.Venable
Aide-de-Camp Col. Charles Marshall
Chief Q/M Col. James L. Corley
Chief of Commisary Col. R. G. Cole
Chief of Ordnance Col. B. G. Baldwin
Asst. Insp. Gen. Col. H. L. Peyton
Chief of Artillery Brig. Gen. W.N. Pendleton
Medical Director Doctor L. Guild
Chief Engineer Col. W. Proctor Smith
Asst. Adj. Gen. Major H. E. Young
Asst. Adj. Gen. Major G. B. Cook [54]

The purpose of a headquarters' staff was all-inclusive: it was to help a commander perform administrative and operational duties and to monitor the condition of troops; it was to expedite actions such as preparing for a march, coordinating an attack, or repelling an assault; it was to assist a commander with everything needed to operate: planning, supplying, surveying, gathering and analyzing information, reporting and updating conditions, and especially communications.

It was physically impossible for a commanding-general to personally witness conditions everywhere in a battle line or to interview directly, subordinate commanders for each pending action. Staff helped maintain at least some form of a commander's presence across the breadth of the army. Confederate Major Samuel W. Melton, Assistant Adjutant-General, wrote on the importance of a commander's staff:

> The staff deserves earnest consideration. My limited experience in the service has been sufficient to convince me that the importance of an efficient staff has been much underestimated, and that it cannot be overestimated. In the work of discipline, in the matters of supply, in the successful pursuit of the campaign, well-nigh everything depends upon a competent, earnest, and laborious staff. The Army is childlike, utterly dependent. The general cannot be ubiquitous--is indeed but a man. The staff must make up the complement. [55]

The Army of the Potomac's staff performance at Gettysburg was a mix between dedicated and heroic men performing great achievements and personnel doing substandard work. There were staff deficiencies when assisting Meade in maneuvering his troops and in communicating critical information. Deficiencies included insufficient monitoring of 3rd Corps placement and subsequent movements on July 2nd. After the war, Col. Thomas Rafferty, Sickles' 3rd Corps at Gettysburg, commented about Meade's staff at Gettysburg:

> My own opinion has always been that the staff of a general commanding the army should be something more than mere clerks to draw up papers and carry messages. Lee's staff was certainly more than this at Gettysburg....Meade's staff were the same officers who for a long time past had been acting in that capacity under previous commanders of the army, and they should have known what was necessary to be done, and the right time and men to do it. They knew well the character and capabilities of the various corps commanders, and which of them were best adapted to accomplish a given result. They should have known all about our line of battle; have made themselves familiar with its salient points, its capabilities for defense or its facilities for offensive operations. They should have directed and controlled the positions of the various corps; should have been the eyes of General Meade, the brains to plan and, under his direction, the hands to execute; should have seen all the enemy proposed to do, and so prepared their own plans as to checkmate and overwhelm him, as with the proper dispositions they might easily have done. But they did none of these things. They knew absolutely nothing of the position of affairs on the left flank (July 2nd); hardly knew whether there was any left flank - certainly did not of their own knowledge as late as 4 o'clock in the day; and yet the position of all others the most vital to the success of our army, nay even to its very existence, was utterly unknown to any of them until General Warren accidentally stumbled upon it. [56]

Col. Rafferty, elaborating on the controversial forward move of Gen. Sickles' 3rd Corps on July 2nd, pointed out the absence of Meade's staff:

> ...The only officer of our army, with the exception of General Meade himself, who ever officially inspected [Sickles' line, was] General Hunt, Chief of Artillery...At the urgent solicitations of General Sickles, and by the consent of General Meade, [Hunt]

> rode out to examine it. It will be remembered that the Third Corps had never been placed in position by any one from headquarters having authority to do so...[57]

Col. Rafferty, of course, gives a partisan view on the controversial forward move of the 3rd Corps on July 2nd. Headquarters staff did make several attempts to communicate instructions with Sickles in order to place his corps in position. Rafferty, nevertheless, makes some reasonable observations on what was expected of a headquarters staff and he points out its shortcomings with regards to its absence in actively monitoring the progress of Sickles' corps in positioning according to instructions. Early on, from the communications between Meade's staff and Sickles, it was obvious Sickles did not have a clear understanding of what ground his corps was to occupy.

Other criticisms regarding the Army of the Potomac's staff performance point to the poor assistance offered to the retreating Union soldiers on July 1st as they fled through Gettysburg seeking a place to rally. The 1st Corps, for example, to get into the battle on McPherson's and Oak Ridge, had skirted the town. In the retreat, many of the soldiers fled through Gettysburg. The troops knew nothing of the town's layout or where the streets funneled.

The retreat was, in itself, no easy feat to accomplish, even under peaceful conditions. The movement involved two infantry corps, the 1st and 11th, concentrating from two directions, towards a collision course with each other in the town with few avenues for movement to the retreat point, Cemetery Hill. Under ideal conditions, this type of maneuver called for organizing a complicated traffic plan to permit a simultaneous and orderly movement of units from the two corps in column formation and, at the same time, keep the two corps from mixing together.

Given the combat conditions in which the movement was made, the two corps moved towards Cemetery Hill in a huge traffic jam of infantrymen, retiring artillery batteries, and wagons. Retreating 1st Corps units collided with 11th Corps troops in the town, stopped their progress, and caused men in the rear to be captured. If two corps commanders, Howard and Doubleday, had any contingent plans for an orderly retreat there is no record of it.[58]

Some staff members from each of the two corps headquarters should have coordinated the retreat, sped up the movement of troops, and directed the way through the labyrinth of side streets, back yards, and alleys to their rallying point on Cemetery Hill. In addition to the above example and to be discussed more later, insufficient staff guidance, on

July 2nd, sent 12th Corps' troops from Culp's Hill to the left flank. The commanders were sent on a movement which lacked basic instructions on the direction to take, the arrival point, and the object of the move.

Staff performance on the Confederate side received criticism as well. Confederate Major Melton noted:

> While it is, and should be esteemed, the most important, I regret to believe that the staff is in our Army the most indifferent feature. Staff officers are as a rule men too young in years, given to levity of mind and conduct, and absorbed in attention to their personal concerns. They are brave and chivalrous young men, daring in action, nothing more; and their daring is not worth the daring of the private soldier--it does not kill, and is worthless as an example, because they have failed elsewhere to inspire respect and confidence. There are many causes for this state of things. While promotion is rapid in the line, it comes scarcely at all in the staff; and if at all it is the incident attending the promotion of the chief, and not the reward of merit.
>
> It is perhaps, in a contest like this, an instance of frailty that men of brains, of enlarged mental and business capacities, will not seek employment, however useful, where there are no rewards; and if they by mistake fall into such employment they are too prompt to leave it for more inviting and promising labors.[59]

Critics of Confederate staff performance also point to a lack of communication early in the campaign that seriously affected the army's movements and directed the Army of Northern Virginia to its ultimate battle site–Gettysburg:

1. During Confederate Gen. Jeb Stuart's cavalry ride behind enemy lines, Gen. Lee was forced to maneuver the bulk of his army in enemy territory without the benefit of intelligence expected from Stuart's detached main force. Perhaps some of the problem was caused by Gen. Lee not making his instructions clear enough to Stuart. However, Stuart's staff, in this case, did not assist with the task for which it was supposed to help – track the Union army and advise Lee of its whereabouts. Additional complications ensued from Stuart's failure to clarify what was expected of the two cavalry brigades [Jones' and Robertson's] left behind and assigned to screen their army's movements and observe the enemy. The result was that two brigades remained in

Virginia when they could have been used valuably elsewhere, perhaps to discover the progress of the Army of the Potomac's movements much sooner than Lee's enlightenment three days before the battle of Gettysburg. Their delayed absence from Lee's forward movements was corrected only after Lee ordered them across the river on July 2nd.[60]

2. On July 2nd, because of failed staff work, Confederate units of Longstreet's corps suffered a serious delay in getting onto the field for that day's assault. In the deployment, Longstreet was under orders from Lee not to be discovered. The route to get to the battle line was not examined properly prior to the march and using it would have disclosed his movements. Changing the route resulted in the infamous countermarch of over 14,000 troops and the start of the assault was delayed until late afternoon. Since the planned attack was to be in stages, the type and scope of the attack required hours to be fully launched. The delayed start restricted the amount of daylight remaining to exploit any advantages gained for troops used in the final stage of the attack.

3. Also on July 2nd, the Confederate attack against the Union right was to be made by two divisions. One division, under Gen. Jubal Early, had to traverse 700 yards to make contact. The other, under Gen. Robert Rodes, was to support Early but it had to advance through Gettysburg, deploy, and cross 1,400 yards to make contact with the enemy. The action was launched without coordination. It resulted in some success for Early but failure for Rodes. Each division lacked the cooperation of the other and allowed the Union forces to make a successful counterattack on Cemetery Hill and regain the ground captured by Early. Staff, in this case, failed to give proper attention to moving two separate forces, each having different considerations of time and distance. Attention to planning in such matters was a basic task expected from the staff function.

Shortcomings of staff performance, on the other hand, were not totally controllable and, most likely, uncontrollables caused some of the problems mentioned in this work. Staff personnel were busiest during combat and could not always meet their commander's needs: they were sent on missions to other parts of the field to confer with other commanders, to wait for units and point out routes of march, to place units in battle lines, to survey ground, to reconnoiter, to prepare maps, and to perform many routine, but necessary, administrative duties. Sudden commitments to a large volume of assignments, each one deemed urgent, overburdened the staff pool and affected its efficiency to accomplish tasks or ignore them altogether.

Most commanders would have preferred more assistance in carrying out their missions. Both armies' chiefs of artillery, Gen. Hunt and Gen. Pendleton, for example, had extensive duties prescribed for them, yet little or no staff was provided to carry out their obligations. Gen. Hunt described this deficiency at Gettysburg:

> My rank, brigadier-general, the command being that of a lieutenant-general, gave me a very small and insufficient staff, and even this had been recently cut down. The inspector of artillery, Lieutenant-Colonel Warner, adjutant-general, Captain Craig, my only aide, Lieutenant Bissell, my one orderly, and even the flag-bearer necessary to indicate my presence to those seeking me, were busy conveying orders or messages, and I was alone; a not infrequent and an awkward thing for a general who had to keep up communications with every part of a battlefield and with the general-in-chief. [61]

If weaknesses were evident in staff performance, it was ultimately the commander's job to establish the quality of performance and a staff size large enough to function adequately. Corrections or contingencies should have been made between battles through self-scrutiny or outside critiques. Commanders, then, should not be completely exonerated because of failures directly related to poor or insufficient staff work. Additionally, with regard to Gettysburg, Lee had the tremendous advantage of having an established working relationship with his staff in the role of commanding-general over the newly appointed Meade, working with Gen. Hooker's old staff.

Communicator Style

A commander's style determined the way orders were communicated for action. Each commander had a different philosophy on the level of detail he wished to convey in his instructions. Each had a different relationship and understanding with which subordinates interpreted instructions.

Meade's communication style at Gettysburg, for example, was an active one. He frequently moved about his lines disregarding the surrounding dangers and made a point of informing important officers of developing situations. As previously mentioned, he valued the involvement of his staff and top commanders, their opinions, and solicited votes on important options for actions during operations. He, with the help of staff officers and corps commanders, moved large masses of troops around every part of the field to head off threats to his battle line.

Meade's active involvement required constant contact with his forces; he realized this at the risk of his own safety. Meade described his involvement during the July 3rd cannonade at his Leister house headquarters:

> Having around me a large number of officers and animals exposed without any particular necessity to the very severe fire, the question of moving my headquarters to a position less exposed, was repeatedly brought to my notice; but in view of the importance of my being, where it was known I could be found, I felt compelled to decline listening to any appeals, till near (as it afterwards proved) the close of the bombardment, when being informed there was a signal officer on the hill [Powers Hill] on the Baltimore Pike (occupied as Headquarters by Major-General Slocum,) who could communicate with the signal officer at the Headquarters I was occupying, I ordered the Headquarters to be transferred to this hill.... On arriving at the hill selected...I then ascertained the signal officer at the house had left there. As soon as I learned this, I returned immediately to my old Headquarters...[62]

Arguably, Meade's greatest accomplishment towards victory at Gettysburg was orchestrating the defensive moves of his army - the timely arrival of men at the right points and in the right strengths to avoid the total collapse of the line. Although some units were misdirected or lost in transit, such as 12th corps units on July 2nd, the arrival of troops at the right time and right place was not all coincidental or luck. Some might judge Meade as having a natural talent for judging the "ripeness" of a battle and knowing when to hold men back or when to commit them in battle. Others may judge Meade's performance, not so much as an exercise in skilled planning, but more by using a crisis management style which simply shoved enough troops around wherever the danger existed, to outlast the attackers and stop a collapse of the line. In any event, timing and skill were crucial to integrating fresh units with ones already in the fray. Too many units in one place, crowded soldiers into jumbled masses of men which blocked fields of fire of friendly troops. Too few units in one place could force men back and trigger a stampede to the rear. [63]

Lee's communication style was different than Meade's. Lee, in speaking of his troop dispositions to an officer, said: "Captain, I do everything in my power to make my plans as perfect as possible, and to bring the troops upon the field of battle; the rest must be done by my generals and their troops, trusting to Providence for the victory." In the estimation of the officer, Lee "would successfully oppose immense odds, as the result of his thorough preparation, so long as he was minutely advised of the whereabouts, strength, and intentions of the enemy." [64]

Gen. Lee exhibited this delegating style at Gettysburg. He laid out his plans, distributed broadly phrased orders to his subordinates, and altered the plan to respond to changes in events. After discussing and finalizing the plan in detail with his commanders, it was left up to them to implement the proposal in their own fashion and arrange any refinements needed to address the nuances and subtleties affecting their battle ground. The impact of Lee's style as a communicator will be discussed later.

Message Origination

Composition of messages required attentiveness in preparation, brevity, completeness, possible contingencies, and timely information. Correctly prepared messages that were concise, clear, and easy to understand, insured that directions would be followed quickly. Care in avoiding the pitfalls of message preparation eliminated mistakes, waste, confusion, and duplication of effort.

If the wording of an order had an incomplete message, if it was vague and ambiguous, and no one would understand the intent, it was not ready for transmission. The text must be examined for flaws and, when it was ready for transmission, the messenger must understand it precisely, be able to repeat an oral order, and ask questions to insure accuracy in transmission. Without these considerations, communication in the chain of command was transmitted not as an organization but as a bunch of words with potentially dangerous consequences. [65]

Aware of the consequences of ambiguity in issuing important orders, Meade's chief of staff, Gen. Daniel Butterfield described his concern over the proper wording of Meade's contingent order in the event of a retreat from Gettysburg:

> After finishing it I presented it to Gen. Meade, and it met his approval. I then stated to him that it would be a great deal better if that order was to be executed, as it might involve grave consequences if not properly executed, to submit it for careful examination to such general officers as were then present, with a view of giving them as opportunity of finding any fault with it then, so that no misunderstanding should arise from the manner in which it was worded or expressed....Some of the officers read it over and said that they thought it was correctly prepared. The order was given to Gen. [Seth] Williams and was copied by the clerks. [66]

Orders were needed in four situations: 1. to start an action. 2. to correct a mistake in an action or solve a problem. 3. to speed up or slow down the action. 4. to stop the action. Written orders from commanders were generally scribbled on paper and sent on their way. Written orders, however, were rare once a battle began.

Instead, verbal orders were rattled off to aides who were sent to different parts of the field, which produced a constant flow of couriers to and from headquarters. Transmitting orders verbally, other than a simple sentence or two, was the least reliable method of communication. The chances of corrupting a message's intent increased if it passed through several transfer points. Complicated messages were prone to garbling in delivery and having their meaning distorted. To insure an accurate transmission, it was important to have a messenger who was capable of delivering the message in the precise context it was created. Napoleon Bonaparte, for example, would call for an aide, give orders slowly and clearly, and each time required it to be repeated. If unsatisfactory, the order was given again in a calm manner, and the aide repeated it again. When successful, the aide was given the "go ahead" and took off. [67]

Frictions in communications had many causes:

At the highest levels of leadership, it is natural to expect commanders to be the best informed, to have access to the best expertise, and to possess the greatest overall picture. But, ignorance of the big picture was not just confined to men in the lower commands. It must be recognized that the headquarters at any command level did not always have the latest and most accurate information to issue orders appropriate to the situation. Union Gen. Doubleday, division/corps commander at

Gettysburg, once aptly remarked: "People are very much mistaken when they suppose because a man is in battle he knows all about it. It is difficult in the excitement of a battle," he noted, "to see everything going on around us for each has his own part to play and that absorbs his attention to the exclusion of everything else." [68]

Conflicting Orders

As in some examples mentioned earlier under the 'command friction' category, conflicting orders placed an immense burden on subordinate officers and their men trying to obey them. "Just before the battle of Five Forks", Joshua Chamberlain wrote, "Within the space of two hours, Warren (commanding 5th Corps) received orders involving important movements for his entire corps, in four different directions. These came in rapid succession. The order which came to General Warren that night were to an amazing degree confused and conflicting....But of course many evil effects of such conditions most naturally fall upon the officer receiving them. Although the responsibility according to military usage and ethics rests upon the officer originating the order, yet the practical effects are apt to fall upon the officer trying to execute it." [69]

Uncertain Instructions

Communiqués were sometimes worded in a manner so indefinite it was unclear whether the message was one of advice or one of command. On June 16th, Gen. Halleck told Gen. Hooker, "There is now no doubt that the enemy is surrounding Harper's Ferry, but in what force I have no information. General Schenck says our force there is much less than before reported, and cannot hold out very long. He wished to know whether he may expect relief. He can hope for none, excepting from your army." Several hours later Halleck added, "....Any troops you can send [for]...relief should be in motion."

From this information Hooker knew Harper's Ferry was surrounded and needed help. Hooker answered accordingly, "In compliance with your directions, I shall march to the relief of Harper's Ferry. I put my column again in motion at 3 a.m. to-morrow. I expect to reach there in two days, and, if possible, earlier."

To Hooker's surprise, Halleck responded. "I have given no directions for your army to move to Harper's Ferry. I have advised the movement of a force, sufficiently strong to meet Longstreet, on Leesburg, to ascertain where the enemy is, and then move to the relief of Harper's Ferry, or elsewhere, as circumstances might require...You are in command of the Army of the Potomac, and will make the particular dispositions as you deem proper. I shall only indicate the objects to be aimed at. We have no positive information of any large force against Harper's Ferry, and it cannot be known whether it will be necessary to go there until you can feel the enemy and ascertain his whereabouts..." [70]

On June 17th Hooker communicated to Halleck: " Advice of the abandonment of Harper's Ferry renders forced marches unnecessary to relieve it." [Whoever advised Hooker of this "abandonment" chose the wrong word in their report.] Halleck responded, "What is meant by abandoning Harper's Ferry is merely that General [Robert] Tyler has concentrated his force in the fortifications on Maryland Heights." Halleck followed this message with, "My telegram of this morning [afternoon] has informed you what is meant by the abandonment of Harper's Ferry--a mere change of position. It changes in no respect the objects you are to keep in view." [71]

Gen. Halleck's initial instructions to Gen. Hooker for sending relief to Harper's Ferry since "there is now no doubt that the enemy is surrounding [it]" appears to more than suggestive advice. Halleck's communications coupled with the confusing use of the term "abandonment" caused unnecessary communication frictions which did not convey the intended meaning for maneuvering the Army of the Potomac during important moments of the campaign.

Insufficient Instructions

On July 2nd, Gen. Slocum sent Gen. Alpheus Williams to lead the 1st division, 12th Corps, Army of the Potomac, to help shore up the collapsing Union left. Williams said:

> We moved around the foot of Power's hill until we struck, as I suppose, the Taneytown Road from which, after moving up it some distance, we struck off to the left in a northwesterly direction, following the sound of the firing which was very heavy just then in that direction. After striking the Taneytown road, we passed large gatherings of our troops swarming in confusion on the easterly slopes of the ridge, apparently recently driven back. A staff officer of General Slocum started with me, but he had no information as to what point reinforcements were needed nor could anyone among the swarming fugitives tell me where I could

> find a corps commander or any organized body of our troops to which I could unite my reinforcements. We were met with loud cheers and shouts to "go on and give them Jessie" but nobody seemed to know where to go in, nor did any of them offer to go in with us. [Williams went in where McGilvery's artillery reserve had made its last stand for the day.] [72]

Gen. John Geary's 2nd division, 12th Corps, also received useless instructions regarding this move. In conjunction with Williams' orders, a large portion of the division lost its direction when transferring from the Union right on Culp's Hill to the army's left flank. "When ordered thus to leave my intrenchments," Geary said, "I received no specific instructions as to the object of the move, the direction to be taken, or the point to be reached, beyond the order to move, by the right flank and to follow the First Division. The First Division having gone out of sight or hearing, I directed the head of my column by the course of some of the men of that division who appeared to be following it." Poor staff assistance, in this case, deprived the Union army of a critical force during a period when the Union line was buckling from the fierce fighting in Sickles' 3rd Corps line. [73]

The portion of Geary's division that left Culp's Hill to help the Union left numbered about 2,500 men. Williams' division numbered over 5,200 men. In this action, about 7,700 men were removed from protecting important ground on Culp's Hill and sent on a mission lacking the most basic information. Williams was under an order which contained no specific destination; it had no specific direction of travel which was eventually discerned only by the sound of gunfire; the staff officer delivering the instructions was passing on a message that was not ready for transmission: the information lacked details and should have been clarified with the sender before relaying them to Williams; there were no high ranking officers at the destination to brief Williams on what he was supposed to do on arrival. [74]

Considering the importance of moving this large body of men during combat, a feat in itself, Williams and Geary deserved more than what they received in terms of information needed to commit their men to a critical point in the battle line. It is not known if Williams actually ended up at the intended destination.

Perhaps Williams and Geary should have insisted on receiving more definite information before the maneuver or circumstances had developed to such an emergency level that their initial orders were simply a desperate move to salvage the situation and patch up the line at any place simply by shoving in manpower. [75]

In a Confederate example, on July 2nd, Major General Richard H. Anderson, 3rd Corps, reported the lack of information and the short notice he received to implement his attack orders: "Shortly after the line had been formed, I received notice that Lieutenant-General [James] Longstreet, 1st Corps, would occupy the ground on the right; that his line would be in a direction nearly at right angles with mine; that he would assault the extreme left of the enemy and drive him toward Gettysburg, and I was at the same time ordered to put the troops of my division into action by brigades as soon as those of General Longstreet's corps had progressed so far in their assault as to be connected with my right flank." The mission assigned to Anderson was not explicit enough to know the precise object of the attack and provided little understanding in recognizing whether the attack before him was going as planned or was a deviation from it. His attack could be characterized more as one of blind purpose than a deliberate and skilled cooperative action trying to outmaneuver the enemy. [76]

Disregarded Orders

Perhaps the best-known disregard of a standing order is the one that sparked the battle of Gettysburg – Gen. Hill's decision to fall upon the Union army against Lee's instruction not to start a general engagement until the army was concentrated.

The meaning of the words "general engagement," as it was used during the Civil War, was one of the terms used to describe different scales of combat. In descending order of conflict size, the scale of combat was termed as a battle, an engagement, a skirmish, an action, and an affair.

The demarcation line that defined an operation as an engagement instead of being called a battle or skirmish is vague. A skirmish entailed light contact with the enemy and, more or less, a disconnected fire. A general engagement was less than a battle when only portions of the army were committed. The increased scale of combat to the status of a battle occurred when armies were fully involved and main lines were locked into combat with full firepower employed and the ability to advance or withdraw was greatly diminished. Since these terms for scales of warfare were indefinite and subjective, it permitted different interpretations which resulted in different actions. Such terms were more appropriately used to describe a past action rather than ones to be used instructively to cause or to refrain from controlling the level of combat in an operation.

Although Lee does not mention the specifics of his order, *not to engage*, in his report, it is verified by others as being the case and not in dispute. Gen. Hill, who Lee was closest to on the march to Gettysburg, also mentioned nothing about Lee's wish not get embroiled in a general engagement [Perhaps Hill was silent on this issue because it was his corps that started the operation which reached the level of a general engagement.]. The day before, on June 30th, however, Gen. James Pettigrew's brigade, part of Hill's 3rd corps, abided by Lee's order when he withdrew from the outskirts of Gettysburg after coming into contact with Gen. Buford's Union cavalry division.

Consequently, on July 1st, Hill intended to advance to Gettysburg with his 3rd corps "and discover what was in my front." This move could have been done with every intention of following Lee's directive. The fighting began around 8 a.m., ending with a lull around noon, when one of Hill's divisions, Heth's, pulled back and disengaged. The move at this point would have been in accordance with Lee's wishes. However, Gen. Ewell's 2nd Corps forces were now arriving on the field from the north. No communication took place between the two corps commands. When the 2nd Corps entered the fray it elevated the scale of battle to the unquestionable level of a general engagement.

If Lee did not want a general engagement he should have communicated this to all corps in the vicinity that were capable of contact with the enemy's main force. Ewell was not made aware of Lee's general engagement instruction until it was too late. Ewell reported:

> I notified the general commanding of my movements, and was informed by him that, in case we found the enemy's force very large, he did not want a general engagement brought on till the rest of the army came up.
>
> By the time this message reached me, General A. P. Hill had already been warmly engaged with a large body of the enemy in his front, and Carter's artillery battalion, of Rodes' division [2nd Corps], had opened with fine effect on the flank of the same body, which was rapidly preparing to attack me, while fresh masses were moving into position in my front. It was too late to avoid an engagement without abandoning the position already taken up, and I determined to push the attack vigorously. [77]

At this stage, Lee's wish to avoid a general engagement was irreversible. According to Gen. Rodes' report "In the midst of the engagement just described [July 1st on Oak Hill], the corps commander [Gen. Ewell] informed me, through one of his officers, that the general commanding did not wish a general engagement brought on, and hence, had it been possible to do so then, I would have stopped the attack at once; but this, of course, it was impossible to do then."

Lee's after-action report said, "It had not been intended to deliver a general battle so far from our base unless attacked, but coming unexpectedly upon the whole Federal Army, to withdraw through the mountains with our extensive trains would have been difficult and dangerous." [Yet, Lee did this right after the battle with his battered army and long trains of wounded.] [78]

The level of action defined by the term "general engagement" in Lee's order was, apparently, broadly interpreted. Despite Gen. Rodes' heavy involvement, at the end of the first day's battle, he was still not convinced that the operation had reached the level of general engagement. Rodes reported:

> [July 1, after the Union retreat]...Before the completion of his defeat before the town, the enemy had begun to establish a line of battle on the heights back of the town, and by the time my line was in a condition to renew the attack, he displayed quite a formidable line of infantry and artillery immediately in my front, extending smartly to my right, and as far as I could see to my left, in front of Early. To have attacked this line with my division alone, diminished as it had been by a loss of 2,500 men, would have been absurd. Seeing no Confederate troops at all on my right; finding that General Early, whom I encountered in the streets of the town within thirty minutes after its occupation by our forces, was awaiting further instructions, and, receiving no orders to advance, though my superiors were upon the ground, I concluded that the order not to bring on a general engagement was still in force, and hence placed my lines and skirmishers in a defensive attitude, and determined to await orders or further movements either on the part of Early or of the troops on my right. [79]

In the final analysis it is difficult to place blame on any one person for appearing to have disregarded Lee's order to avoid a general engagement. Once the first shot was fired it was difficult to overcome the dynamics of combat: 1.Hill started the action but disengaged. 2.

Ewell's men entered the action unaware of Lee's order. 3. Hill re-engaged to help Ewell.

The confusion in the term "general engagement," nevertheless, has been attached to Gen. Hill's reputation ever since the battle. Hill's "disregard" of Lee's order is one of the many tenets applied to explain Lee's loss at Gettysburg. However, at the point when Lee finally arrived on the field, mid-afternoon on July 1st, the command and responsibility for prolonging any operation shifted from Hill or Ewell to the commanding-general. Lee could have ascribed to his own order and withdrew his forces. But choosing, instead, to remain and allow the fight to intensify was the defining moment which committed the Army of Northern Virginia to its eventual defeat.

While it may be perceived that, at the end of the first day's fight, Lee was unalterably committed to battle because of the actions of subordinate commanders, the Army of Northern Virginia was not irretrievably stuck in a position and unable to move back: The Union forces present were in complete disarray and, even from Lee's view of the action, were incapable of mounting a counterattack; the later-formed fishhook lines of both armies were not even in the beginning stages of being shaped; Lee had a full day to decide whether to stay or withdraw; all of Lee's wagons were not yet on the Gettysburg side of the mountains; there was enough good ground for a defensive withdrawal through Cashtown Pass.

Had Lee withdrawn his army after the victorious first day, A. P. Hill's decision to start the battle might have been deemed brilliant and praiseworthy of initiative: Hill caught the Union army off guard when he had the advantage of greater manpower and better position to maneuver; the enemy was not concentrated; Hill and Ewell jointly exploited enemy weaknesses before the Army of the Potomac could build enough strength to fight effectively. More than likely, a one-day-only encounter at Gettysburg would have provoked a battle elsewhere since both armies were close to each other and the concentration of each force was nearly complete. Nevertheless, disengaging the Army of Northern Virginia after that first day's triumphant action would have, at least, established Generals Hill and Ewell as the victors of Gettysburg.

On July 1st, when Gen. Lee saw the Union army tumbling off Seminary Ridge in total confusion, he saw victory [perhaps a decisive win to end the war] and knew what demoralizing effects would be cast upon his troops if he turned around and retreated in the face of triumph.

Orders with Difficult Prerequisites

There is a "part two" connected with Lee's use of the term "general engagement." In Gen. Lee's after action report, he detailed his instructions on rules of engagement following the Union retreat through Gettysburg on July 1st:

> It was ascertained from the prisoners that we had been engaged with two corps of the army formerly commanded by General Hooker, and that the remainder of that army, under General Meade, was approaching Gettysburg. Without information as to its proximity, the strong position which the enemy had assumed could not be attacked without danger of exposing the four divisions present, already weakened and exhausted by a long and bloody struggle, to overwhelming numbers of fresh troops. General Ewell was, therefore, instructed to carry the hill occupied by the enemy, if he found it practicable, but to avoid a general engagement until the arrival of the other divisions of the army, which were ordered to hasten forward. He decided to await Johnson's division..."

In this report, Lee gave instructions to Ewell which contained two prerequisites: 1.Take the hill "if he found it practicable." 2. "Avoid a general engagement." Lee's report recognized that the enemy held a strong position with "overwhelming numbers of fresh troops." In the final analysis, the desired degree of contact with enemy forces could not be regulated once the fight was underway. Avoiding a general engagement required the cooperation of both sides. Gen. Ewell must have been puzzled in trying to figure out how to follow Lee's directive - to take a hill packed with enemy troops, yet avoid a general engagement.[80]

Poor or Incorrect Wording

With just a few simple phrases of poorly chosen words, orders could confound and mislead subordinate commanders attempting to obey them. Gen. Sickles, to help shore up his vulnerable 3rd Corps line on July 2nd, secured permission from headquarters to draw *support* from Caldwell's division of the 2nd Corps and borrow a brigade from Gen. Sykes' 5th Corps. Sykes recognized his *support* mission "should it be required."

Soon afterwards, however, Sykes received a message from Meade to "throw all his corps to the Union left and to hold it at *all hazards*." From this directive, Sykes' mission changed from a *supporting role* to help Sickles to one of a *commanding role* responsible for holding the Union left. This left Sykes no other choice than to believe that he was relieved of any supporting obligations to the 3rd Corps. "Hold it at all hazards" was an indisputable instruction to *direct* the action. [Emphases added.]

While all this was happening, Gen. Sickles and Gen. Birney, 3rd Corps division commander, continued to believe and to rely on the 5th Corps in a supporting role. Through Meade's permission, in their view, they considered the 5th Corps to be subordinate to the 3rd Corps commander and, therefore, subject to Sickles' orders. The dual misunderstanding of two corps commanders, operating in the same combat area and each believing to be in charge, created a needless crisis at the most inopportune moment. As 5th Corps troops arrived at the front, 3rd Corps staff officers desperately sought Sykes' assistance. Sykes naturally rebuffed their pleas for help since it was Meade who entrusted him to hold the line at "all hazards." The stalemate was partially broken by the fortunate arrival of the 6th Corps upon which Meade ordered the 5th Corps to the left and assigned them as a reserve [Coddington's *The Gettysburg Campaign* said, "Presumably...as an autonomous unit...rather than to be used in a piecemeal fashion to bolster the Third Corps."] Nevertheless, Sickles and Birney still continued to order up 5th Corps units for use with the 3rd Corps. [81]

On July 4th, in General Order #68, Meade thanked the Army of the Potomac for their valiant victory at Gettysburg: "Our task is not yet accomplished, and the commanding-general looks to the army for greater efforts to drive from our soil every vestige of the presence of the invader." [82]

On July 6th, Lincoln communicated to Gen. Halleck in reference to Meade's General Order: "You know I did not like the phrase, in Orders, No. 68, I believe, 'Drive the invaders from our soil.' Since that, I see a dispatch from General [William] French, saying the enemy is crossing his wounded over the river in flats, without saying why he does not stop it, or even intimating a thought that it ought to be stopped." Lincoln, at this point highly concerned, felt Meade's timid moves were allowing "to get the enemy across the river again without a further collision, and they do not appear connected with a purpose to prevent his crossing and to destroy him…"

Lincoln's closing remark to Halleck stated, "If you are satisfied the latter purpose is entertained and is judiciously pursued, I am content. If you are not so satisfied, please look to it." [83]

Meade's misspoken words were, perhaps, more of a harmless slip of the tongue – an expression of relief and an end to an especially bloody and decisive battle rather than a commander's satisfaction that the campaign ended the conflict. Perhaps too much was placed in the meaning of his words. It was written by a man who just experienced the greatest mental challenge of his life, a man who was given the sole responsibility of saving his nation on the brink of disaster. Meade's words, nevertheless, nettled his superiors enough for them to fire back communications to insure he understood the game plan. But Meade's mood in reacting to the riling tone of the messages from Washington prompted the commanding-general to offer his resignation.

Meade's pursuit of Lee's retreating army raised further scrutiny regarding the pace at which he moved. Despite questions raised on this issue, even today, Meade did proceed with his tattered army in tailing Lee towards the Potomac River. He moved with a degree of caution, however, not as a victorious general bent on destroying the enemy during one of its weakest moments. On July 6th, he ordered Gen. Sedgwick, then acting as a wing commander, to move accordingly: "With this disposition of three corps under your immediate command, and two within support,... I am of the opinion that you are in a measure secure on your right flank and rear, and, therefore, can examine the front. All evidence seems to show a movement to Hagerstown and the Potomac...I apprehend *they will be likely to let you alone, if you let them alone*." The same day, Gen. Warren, acting as Meade's chief of staff, gave similar non-confrontational orders to Gen. Thomas Neill, brigade commander, Sedgwick's corps. Warren said, "The object of detaching you from General Sedgwick's corps is to have you *watch closely* the movements of the enemy's rear guard, and inform the commanding-general frequently." [emphases added]

Meade's choices of words in his orders were ones of caution: to "let them alone" and to "watch closely." Meade, however, had any number of reasons to proceed the way he did. Having been in the position of commanding-general for little more than a week, he spent most of his tenure leading his army by crisis management: he fixed problems defensively rather than aggressively causing them for the enemy. Meade was well aware that the Army of the Potomac had just ended a long string of losing battles and that recently winning "one in a row" did not firmly establish his army's reputation as being unbeatable. Meade also had a tired and wounded army of men and animals, broken equipment, short supplies, and his forces were moving in poor weather.

Perhaps more importantly, Meade was still under instructions from his superiors to operate with a defensive view – to protect Washington and Baltimore. Thus, Meade's primary basis for his course of action was defensive and, at the same time, to reposition his supply lines to replenish his depleted army. Yet, he was also expected to act aggressively towards pursuing the defeat of Lee's army. The nature of his mostly defensive assignment reduced his choices for maneuvering. For the time being, it was appropriate for Meade to operate in a defensive manner and not tinker with an enemy force until the fighting spunk of his adversary was determined. Besides, operating with a defensive stance made it especially difficult to force an engagement and defeat an enemy which was attempting to move away from the Army of the Potomac. While Meade did not deliberately allow Lee to escape across the Potomac River, the fact that he did increased the chances of success in his mission - defending Washington and Baltimore. The river added a major obstacle by preventing the Army of Northern Virginia from threatening these two cities. [84]

Discretionary orders

The Civil War introduced a new era which involved large operations where commanding-generals lost direct control of their forces. Commanding-generals operated with huge numbers of troops, battle lines miles long, and covered large areas of terrain. They could no longer rely on staff officers alone to manage operations. The use of discretionary orders to subordinate field commanders was one method of overcoming the lack of direct control.

When Gen. Lee headed northward to Pennsylvania, he issued discretionary orders when he discovered that the Union army had crossed the Potomac. He instructed Gen. Ewell to march on Cashtown or Gettysburg, "according to circumstances." Gen. Isaac Trimble's later recollection of Lee's order indicated, first, a perplexed group of the high command trying to decipher Lee's intention and, second, a group anxious for more direction. Trimble wrote:

> In the evening Gen. Ewell called in Rhodes [sic], Early, and Trimble for consultation. Read over the order of Gen'l Lee several times, commenting on its "indefinite

> phraseology," as he expressed it, in very severe terms, and asking each one what was meant by "according to circumstance." Gen'l Early and Rhodes gave unsatisfactory opinions when Gen'l Trimble spoke and said, "I think I can fully explain the words" according to circumstances. [Trimble, from an earlier conversation with Lee, explained that, he intended to fall on the enemy's advance. Trimble believed citizens' reports that the 1st Corps was already in Gettysburg.] "...That is the circumstance which directs you to march on that place...This explanation did not satisfy Gen'l Ewell, who more than once patiently remarked, 'Why can't a commanding-general have someone of his staff who can write an intelligible order?' "[85]

On the morning of July 1st at Gettysburg, discretionary orders were vital to introducing and engaging troops in this unplanned action. The battle started without the presence of either commanding-general - Lee was in Cashtown, eight miles away and Meade was still in Maryland, ten miles distant. Without detailed knowledge of the ground and the disposition of enemy forces, Meade and Lee could gather information only as fast as men on horseback could move. Until more precise information was gained about the enemy location and intentions, the disposition of friendly forces, and the lay of the land, commanding-generals could issue orders to their field commanders only of an indefinite nature. Discretionary orders, then, were necessary until the situation clarified.

Discretionary orders provided wonderful opportunities for leadership. Each commanding-general had issued discretionary orders to their respective senior officers. Union Gen. Reynolds, left wing commander, was sent forward to look over the ground at Gettysburg and decide whether it was suitable for giving battle. He was given the discretion of staying or retiring towards Taneytown, Md. At the close of battle on July 1st, Gen. Ewell was given that well-known discretionary order to take the high ground "if practicable."

The merits of the final choices made by a commander under discretionary orders can only be viewed in hindsight. If the choice worked out, the general, of course, was a good leader; and if it failed, he was a poor one. Furthermore, if the discretionary choice of a commander ended with poor results, it is almost always concluded that the alternative choice would have been successful and always better, but never worse, than the choice that failed.

A pertinent point, however, was the fact that discretionary orders were a transfer of a superior officer's responsibility to a subordinate. The transfer of responsibility added an uncertainty – it created an additional risk by giving others the opportunity to choose a path of action normally reserved for the superior and permitted the initiation of important events without his supervision.

Proficient commanders, therefore, issued discretionary orders only in situations where leaders had a solid trust in their subordinates' judgment. A case in point, discussed earlier, was Meade giving Gen. Hancock the temporary field command over other senior commanders.

Or, in another rather exceptional case regarding the Pickett/Pettigrew/Trimble assault on July 3rd, Gen. Longstreet issued a discretionary order to Col. E. P. Alexander, artillery battalion commander, giving him the responsibility of judging when the artillery had done its damage and signaling when the infantry attack was to begin. Longstreet said:

> If the artillery fire does not have the effect to drive off the enemy or greatly demoralize him, so as to make our effort pretty certain, I would prefer that you should not advise Gen. [George] Pickett to make the charge. I shall rely a great deal upon your good judgment to determine the matter, and shall expect you to let Gen. Pickett know when the moment offers. [86]

Alexander was, undoubtedly, surprised to have himself, a mere colonel, assigned to such a weighty responsibility for the destiny of 12,000 men. After the exchange of several messages clarifying the wording of the order, Alexander diplomatically refused to accept this trust by responding, "General: When our artillery fire is at its best, I will advise Gen. Pickett to advance." [87]

Another example involves Lee's directive on July 1st, to take the high ground "if practicable." Although covered earlier in reference to orders with prerequisites, it is discussed here with respect to the order's discretionary nature. Even though the phraseology of Lee's order was indefinite, it expressed Lee's definite desire to take the hill. The wording of the order entrusted to Ewell the decision to carry out Lee's preference. Ewell had already been engaged in the fight; as a result, he knew more about the battle at this point than Lee. Ewell must have weighed the circumstances. After long hours of marching and fighting, did his troops have enough strength to continue the fight? What losses had they suffered already? How many Union men were defending that high ground? How much artillery was present? How could an attack be made on streets perpendicular to the enemy? Considering these questions, plus a report that the enemy was advancing on his left, Ewell concluded he could not bring his artillery to bear on the objective, Cemetery Hill. The hill was not assailable from the town, and he chose to halt.[88]

The lost opportunities from Ewell's decision to halt are well known. If Lee considered that the possession of the Union high ground was of the utmost importance he could just have easily rephrased his order to take the high ground at all costs. But to second guess the judgment of one of his corps commanders was not Lee's style. With hindsight, Ewell's circumstances prompting his decision to halt on July 1st are defensible. Some of his men marched twelve miles before engaging in the attack. A number of troops were needed to round up and remove thousands of Union prisoners just captured. The town itself interfered with coordinating the Confederate assault and disrupted the advance as much as it did in the Union withdrawal. Additionally, troops already engaged could not fight continuously without stopping to clean muskets or replenish ammunition. Without the presence of Jeb Stuart's cavalry, it was not known if the entire Army of the Potomac was waiting to receive the Confederate advance.

Confederate Col. E. P. Alexander expressed his frustration over the use of indefinite directives: "The words 'if practicable' are always of such doubtful interpretation they should be excluded from all important orders. They leave matters in doubt. Every order should be distinctly either the one thing or the other. Lee used the phrase at Gettysburg, in ordering Ewell to press a routed enemy, and lost his victory by it."[89]

Some orders, however, were termed discretionary when they were really not. If there were no options, then the directive was a firm command. For example, Longstreet's countermarch was not a discretionary action. Failed planning caused the turnaround and, under orders from Lee not to be discovered, Longstreet had no choice but to find an alternate route onto the battlefield.

Gen. Longstreet also received censure for his role in the grand assault on July 3rd. To this he responded:

> It has been said that I should have exercised discretion and should not have sent Pickett on his charge. It has been urged

that I had exercised discretion on previous occasions. It is true that at times when I saw a certainty of success in another direction, I did not follow the orders of my general, but that was when he was not near and could not see the situation as it existed. When your chief is away, you have a right to exercise discretion; but if he sees everything that you see, you have no right to disregard his positive and repeated orders, and when, after discussion he has ordered the execution of his policy. I had offered my objection to Pickett's battle and had been overruled, and I was in the immediate presence of the commanding-general when the order was given for Pickett to advance. [90]

Failed Notification

Orders or instructions were accompanied by certain assumptions necessary for their implementation. For orders directing troop movements, as an example, it was expected that someone knowledgeable would be provided to show the way [Examples discussed earlier.]. If a commander moved from a line, adjacent commanders would be notified; if taken out of a battle line, replacement units would fill in the position.

Before the battle of Gettysburg began, Gen. Buford's Union cavalrymen were exhausted. Many of their horses were unserviceable from the high-paced movements in tracking Lee's army northward. The entire division was due for a much needed rest and re-supply. Before that would happen, the division engaged the Confederates on July 1st. On July 2nd, the men were assigned to protect the left flank of the army, a critical task in acting as an early warning system. Buford's commander, Gen. Alfred Pleasonton communicated to Gen. Meade that Buford's division was in need of refitting. Meade agreed and allowed it to leave the field, assuming, however, that Pleasonton would find a replacement force to take over this important mission. For some unknown reason this was not done. When Meade found out that no replacement was made, it was too late for the problem to be fixed before the action commenced.

The result of this oversight was incalculable and directly due to poor staff work. Lack of cavalry protection was one of the chief reasons why Gen. Sickles moved his 3rd Corps forward from the main battle line. His move prompted the greatest reshuffling of Union troops during the three-day action, the action was the largest engagement of troops in the battle, and resulted in the most casualties. It can be said that failed notifications played a major role in the battle's outcome. It was an oversight that didn't have to happen. [91]

The movement of the 3rd Corps on July 2nd, away from the main Union line, was done without Sickles conferring with the commander of his adjacent force [Gen. Hancock]. Sickles moved far beyond his intended position assigned by Meade. In doing so, he created a large gap and allowed the left flank of Gen. Hancock's 2nd Corps to go unprotected as well as exposing his own line to the dangers of enemy flank attacks. And he moved away from his support. Before the Confederate attack could be halted, the result of the move created a near disaster in the southern half of the Union line.

If Sickles disclosed his forward move to Hancock beforehand, it might have at least allowed Hancock to make contingencies to cooperate with Sickles' action or to support him, if needed. Disclosure to Hancock, beforehand, might also have allowed Sickles' plan to reach Meade's attention before it was implemented, and permitted an opportunity for cancellation.

Another lapse of communication occurred on July 3rd. General William Pendleton, Lee's chief of artillery, borrowed nine of A. P. Hill's howitzers for use with Col. E. P. Alexander's artillery in the assault of Pickett's division. At the right moment, they were to spring into action with Pickett's infantry. When it was time to bring them onto the field, however, they had disappeared. Pendleton had ordered some to the rear and others had their positions changed to avoid the shelling. In doing so, their new location was not communicated to Alexander. This missing firepower, according to Gen. Longstreet, "thus deranged this wise plan." It gave Alexander a sobering surprise as the Confederate infantry columns were put into motion for the assault. Longstreet added, "Never was I so depressed as upon that day." [92]

Cutoff Communication

Following the replacement of Gen. Hooker as commanding-general, Meade's telegraphic communication with Washington and links to surrounding military departments were cut off. Thanks to Jeb Stuart's Confederate cavalry, telegraph lines were destroyed for miles. Meade anxiously attempted to restore his communication links. From a dispatch found on the body of Union soldier killed on June 30th , 4 ½ miles from

Glen Rock, Pa., there was a message from Meade to Halleck, dated 6/29/63:

> I have hastily made up this dispatch to give you the information. Telegraphic communications have been cutoff, I have no opportunity to receive a reply to mine asking your advice as to these movements, and upon my best judgment proceed to execute them. I can at present give no orders as to Gen. Schenck's department in Baltimore, or the Potomac in my rear; neither can I, in the absence of telegraphic communication, and on account of the great distance of Couch, exercise any influence, by advice or otherwise, concerning the cooperation of that force. These circumstances are beyond my control. I send this by courier, with the hope and expectation that it will reach you safely.[93]

Meade asked Gen. Couch in Harrisburg, Pa. if he was able to contact Philadelphia, Baltimore, or Washington and to forward his dispatch to Washington requesting supplies and shoes. Meade, then, had to send messages north to Harrisburg, Pennsylvania, to be rerouted east and south, around damaged telegraph lines until they reached Washington. Arguably, Stuart's greatest success in his ill-fated ride around the Union army was severely limiting the transfer of information and intelligence needed for Meade to react to enemy movements.

Conversely, by cutting off Meade's communication, Stuart was also severing contact with his own army that was waiting to gather the same kind of information and intelligence of which he deprived Meade. The tradeoff did not seem worth the effort - it caught Lee off guard by losing track of the enemy and forced the battle of Gettysburg. For most of the battle, it deprived Lee of Stuart's cavalry for reconnaissances and counterbalancing the Union cavalry. And Stuart's ride placed his exhausted men and horses into a condition unsuitable for combat. In his after action report Stuart said:

> Reaching Dover, Pa., on the morning of July 1, I was unable to find our forces. The most I could learn was that General Early had marched his division in the direction of Shippensburg, which the best information I could get seemed to indicate as the point of concentration of our troops. After as little rest as was compatible with the exhausted condition of the command, we pushed on for Carlisle, where we hoped to find a portion of the

army. I arrived before that village, by way of Dillsburg, in the afternoon.... The whereabouts of our army was still a mystery; but, during the night, I received a dispatch from General Lee (in answer to one sent by Major [Andrew] Venable from Dover, on Early's trail), that the army was at Gettysburg, and had been engaged on this day (July 1) with the enemy's advance. [94]

Encryption Problems

Meade encountered another communication friction dealing with telegraphic messages:

Meade to Halleck, 7/3: "The dispatches from you yesterday owing to the disappearance of Caldwell, telegraph operator here, are here in cipher unintelligible."

Butterfield to Maj. Thomas Eckert, 7/4: "General Meade desires to know under whose orders and authority the telegraph operators possessing the cipher are appointed and controlled. The operator, Mr. Caldwell, at these headquarters presumes to act in an independent manner, and has left hdqtrs, without authority or permission. The commanding-general is unable to send dispatches from these headquarters in cipher in consequence thereof, or to understand those he receives." [95]

Communication Transmission

Joshua Chamberlain wrote: "Rapidly changing plans and movements in affecting the single purpose for which battle is delivered are what a soldier must expect; and the ability to form them wisely and promptly illustrates and tests military capacity…Orders had to pass through many hands; and in the difficulties of delivery owing to distance and the nature of the ground, the situation which called for them had often changed." [96]

Speed, distance, and manpower were important factors affecting the transmission of communications:

Speed

During combat, situations changed rapidly. Communications were slowed down or stopped altogether. The slowness of communicating tested the independent judgment of subordinate commanders: it isolated them from their superior, allowed opportunities for creativity, caused standing orders to be altered or disregarded, and produced different reactions to similar situations.

Military historian Paddy Griffith offers a chart indicating the slow pace in which the chain of command transmitted orders. He acknowledges that this was but a "rough guide," yet it points out the time consumed in communicating within an army:

Typical Message Times

Army commander to Corps HQ	1 hour
Corps HQ to Division HQ	30 minutes
Division HQ to Brigade HQ	20 minutes
Brigade HQ to Regimental HQ	15 minutes
Regimental HQ to Company Commander	5 minutes
Company Commander to Enlisted Men	1 minute [97]

To understand any military action more clearly, students of battles must consider the element of transmission time in the analysis and judgment of how orders were expedited. In doing so, it helps explain why battle plans became obsolete with real time conditions and why actions frequently did not follow the intended plan. Using the above "rough guide," attacks, then, were not launched just with rousing yells of "come on, boys!" Assaults, especially large scale ones, required a painful amount of time to position forces at staging areas, to deploy them into battle formations, to communicate orders to officers, to shout inspirational words of encouragement to long lines of men, and finally, to move forward. [98]

Distance

In 21st century warfare, the factors of time and distance affecting communications have been conquered by technology. In the Civil War, however, these factors won and lost battles. While messages could be delivered on foot at short distances, commanders making the decisions needed access to observation points and quick access to their superiors and subordinates.

Oliver Norton, Vincent's brigade, Union 5th corps, gives us some insight on ground covered on July 2nd in the tense moments surrounding the attack against Little Round Top:

> No private soldier in the 5th Corps, knowing the distances that Sykes [5th Corps commander] and Barnes [5th Corps division commander] had to traverse that day, would believe that they went about on foot. My own recollection is that both were well mounted and accompanied by the mounted officers of their respective staffs and a number of mounted orderlies. A corps or division commander in the immediate presence of the enemy, wishing to get a better view, might temporarily dismount to be less conspicuous; but he could not properly handle his corps or division by going about on foot....
>
> I believe that Warren did not leave the hill after he reached the signal station until he went down and detached O'Rorke's regiment. Warren had with him that day three lieutenants of engineers serving on his staff, MacKenzie, Reese, and Roebling, also some mounted orderlies.... Warren used these officers of his staff to keep in touch with Meade and take such measures as in his judgment seemed necessary. [99]

In addition, mid-level commanders controlled battle lines far beyond their ability to shout orders or gesture directives. Imagine a brigade of 1,500 men in an attack formation. The brigadier general must survey his line which, when deployed for battle, was longer than five football fields; he must communicate individually to the four or five regiments that make up the brigade. To accomplish this feat, the general must be mounted and he, or an aide, must communicate orders by riding up and down the line from one unit to another.

Take away the brigadier's horse and the impact on communicating had the same effect as demoting the general to a captain commanding a company [one-tenth of a regiment]. This effect happened. On July 3rd, an order was issued that traditionally mounted personnel were to go in on foot in the Pickett/Pettigrew/Trimble assault. Typically, the assault would have used up to two-hundred men on horseback [For various reasons the order to go in on foot was ignored and twenty-five officers and aides were mounted in the attack].

With the exception of the immediate vicinity, the dismounted officers, in effect, deprived their forces of much of its leadership. On the other hand, mounted officers were prime targets for sharpshooters. As a consequence, they were more likely to be injured or killed and so the loss of leadership occurred anyhow. Therefore, in combat, the functions of command and communication were severely reduced when coordinating actions of multiple units. [100]

Manpower

Transmission distance, urgency for information, and the number of message recipients help determine the manpower needed to communicate. To supply the Army of the Potomac, for example, depots in Baltimore and Frederick shipped stores to Westminster, Maryland while Gen. Rufus Ingalls, U.S. Army, Chief Quartermaster, arrived at Gettysburg to coordinate the issuance of supplies to the Army of the Potomac. To maintain a functional system, supply points were in telegraphic communications with other supply points and the Army of the Potomac, in turn, communicated every three hours with Westminster, Md., twenty-five miles away, with a relay system using cavalry couriers. [101]

Shorter lines of communication, of course, simplified matters considerably and normally needed fewer men to perform their tasks. But even here, circumstances to expedite communications could place great burdens on the manpower pool. On July 4th, Gen. Birney, newly appointed commander of the Union 3rd Corps, was ordered to send out a reconnaissance force to locate enemy positions and to provide frequent updates to Gen. Meade. Besides the reconnaissance force itself, the temporary communications link to update Meade took one staff officer along with twenty orderlies. [102]

The Human Factor: Message Corruption/Misunderstood Orders

"...Too often we forget about the 'human systems' that make or break us." [Maureen Burke, manager of training, Coca-Cola Enterprises, Inc.] [103]

Making the right command decisions depended on thoroughness in obtaining accurate information from the field. Implementing orders from those decisions depended on preserving the intent of the orders when conveyed to recipients. Verbal messages, especially during combat, were vulnerable to misunderstanding. During the defense of Little Round Top, on July 2nd, Lt. Col. Norval Welch, commanding the 16th Michigan infantry, described such a case:

> We remained in this position nearly half an hour, when someone (supposed to be General [Stephen] Weed or Major-General Sykes) called from the extreme crest of the hill to fall back nearer the top, where a much less exposed line could be taken up. This order was not obeyed, except by single individuals. From some misconstruction of orders, and entirely unwarrantable assumption of authority, Lieutenant Kydd ordered the colors back. None left with them, however, but three of the color-guard. [104]

Verbally transmitting information accurately required qualified men capable of memorizing instructions and the astuteness to convey the message's purpose. Passing on verbal orders exactly in the manner they originated could not be taken lightly.

In the excitement of battle it was especially challenging. Col. Clark Baldwin, 1st Mass, encountered a mis-communication on July 2nd as the enemy advanced and his unit, then acting as skirmishers, fell back to the main line [Skirmishers typically reform in the rear of the main line and act as support.]:

> I was directing the men as they came in to form in rear of the line of battle, that I might be ready to move to the support of any point necessary; but before reaching the brigade line I received an order from a Staff officer to form my regt. in "front" of the 26th Pa. Regt. The order surprised me and thinking I must have misunderstood the order I asked if I was to form in front of the 26th Pa., the officer replied yes. Still thinking it was wrong, I asked who gave the order, and was told it came from Gen. Carr; thinking that it must be so, but knowing no military rule for such a move I could not understand it but formed my regt. in obedience to the order. At this time the enemy's front line of battle appeared on the rise of ground in our front and poured a terrible volley into our ranks, "killing fire," and wounding twenty-three officers and men...
>
> [On July 3rd] I waited upon Gen. Carr, and informed him of the orders I received from one of his aids [sic] the day before, to form my skirmishers in the front of his line, and asked him if that was his order. He replied, certainly not, my order was for you to form in the rear of the regt. on the right, and prevent the enemy from turning the right flank, should they attempt it; He asked me

> which one of his aides gave me the order, I told him, he replied, what a lunk head he is, I am nearly out of patience with his blunders and I very much regret it, as it cost you the loss of so many good men. [105]

Another costly communication blunder took place on July 3rd during the Union attempt to retake positions lost on Culp's Hill. Gen. Thomas Ruger, 12th Corps brigade commander, requested permission to ascertain the force of the enemy, before making the full attack:

> This was approved by Gen. Slocum. I then sent orders by a staff officer (Lieut. Wm. M. Snow...) to Gen. [sic] [Silas] Colgrove whose brigade was on the right, to advance a line of skirmishers (the enemy had none out, nor ourselves at the time) and if it was found that the enemy held the line only by a skirmish line or weak line, to attack at once with the two regts. [2nd Mass. and 27th Ind.] and take position, but if it held a force not to attempt it....To my surprise, instead of the skirmish line I expected to see, two regts., the 2d Mass. Vols. and 27th Ind. moved out to charge the enemy, came quickly under fire from the enemy still in full force and were repulsed. There was no time to correct the mistake or prevent the result. General Colgrove I knew to be an officer who would know the difference between finding the enemy still strong at the point or sensibly weakened and thought at first that he had intentionally disregarded my order to ascertain the strength of the enemy before making the charge; the more so as he was not only a brave officer but also impetuous. He asserted, however, that he received an order to charge the position with two regts., without condition.
>
> The staff officer maintained that he delivered the order as I gave it, and so I said to him there as no doubt as several heard it. No person heard all that passed between Genl. Colgrove and the Staff Officer, and it was impossible to ascertain which was responsible for the mistake. I concluded at the time and still believe that it was one of those unfortunate occurrences that will happen in the excitement of battle. [106]

On July 2nd, Gen. Joseph Kershaw was moving his brigade of South Carolinians across the Emmitsburg Road to attack the Union guns along the Wheatfield Road and the Union infantry line along the Stony Hill.

Numerous obstacles rendered his line in poor order. Kershaw said, "In order to restore the line of the directing battalion (the Seventh South Carolina), as soon as we reached the cover of the hill, I moved it a few paces by the right flank. Unfortunately, this order given only to Colonel [D. Wyatt] Aiken, was extended along the left of the line, and checked its advance." Kershaw reported: [107]

> After passing the buildings at Rose's, the charge of the left wing was no longer visible from my position; but the movement was reported to have been magnificently conducted until the [Union] cannoneers had left their guns and the caissons were moving off, when the order was given to "move *by the right flank*," by some unauthorized person, and was immediately obeyed by the men. The Federals returned to their guns and opened on these doomed regiments a raking fire of grape and canister, at short distance, which proved most disastrous, and for a time destroyed their usefulness. Hundreds of the bravest and best men of Carolina fell, victims of this fatal blunder. [108]

Kershaw initiated the flank order but it was intended for only one regiment. It was inadvertently transmitted by other officers along the entire left wing causing the deadly result.

At the Wheatfield on July 2nd, Union Col. Jacob Sweitzer, brigade commander, 5th corps, described a near misunderstanding of an order issued in the heat of the fight:

> When the attack commenced, word was sent by General [James] Barnes that *when* we retired we should fall back under cover of the woods. This order was communicated to Colonel [George] Prescott [32nd Mass.] whose regiment was then under the hottest fire. Understanding it to be a peremptory order to retire then, he replied, "I don't want to retire; I am not ready to retire; I can hold this place," and he made good his assertion. Being informed that he misunderstood the order, which was only intended to inform him how to retire when it became necessary, he was satisfied, and he and his command held their ground manfully. [Emphasis added.] [109]

Had Prescott not been so hesitant in following the initial order, as he understood it, withdrawal of his unit might have begun a collapse of the Stony Hill/Wheatfield line sooner than it did.

In one case, an unintentional recipient acted upon information intended for others. Col. Wainright, commanding 1st Corps artillery brigade, reported:

> Having heard incidentally some directions given to General Doubleday about holding Cemetery Hill and not knowing that there was such a place, while the seminary was called indiscriminately cemetery and seminary, I supposed the latter was meant. I therefore directed Captain [James] Cooper to take a good position in front of the professor's house on this ridge, and sent an order to Captain [Greenleaf] Stevens of the Fifth Maine Battery, to occupy the position first assigned to Lieutenant [James] Stewart.... An order was now received by Captain Stevens from General [James] Wadsworth to withdraw his battery. Not knowing that he had received such an order and still under the false impression as to the importance attached to holding Seminary Hill, I directed all batteries to remain in position. A few minutes, however, showed me our infantry rapidly retreating to the town. All batteries were at once limbered to the rear…but it was too late to save everything. [110]

Discipline to Follow Orders

In *Battle Tactics of the Civil War*, Paddy Griffith described the attention commanders needed in order to maintain discipline during combat:

> When a general needs to improve control the general will seek to maintain control of events by sending orders to correct the discrepancies which have developed, and he may even intervene personally to rally a shaky unit….He may jump lustily into the heart of the fight, or he may keep above it cold and aloof. Whichever technique he applies, however, there will come a moment when he realizes that the troops engaged with the enemy in the front line are effectively beyond his control. Their ordeal will have become so much their own affair that they can no

> longer be ordered forward into increased danger, nor be moved sideways or rearwards without the risk of a panic rout. [111]

Combat created a dynamic situation with a life of its own. Any effort applied to make adjustments, even on a small scale, risked the chance of degrading the situation even further, if line adjustments were not made in concert. Men in a battle line tended to stay there because other units were there as well. Any unexplained movement by adjacent units of a line could trigger an unstoppable stampede to the rear. [112]

Federal General John Gibbon, in Washington D. C., April 1st, 1864, testified on the influence of combat upon the discipline of soldiers to follow orders just after Pickett's Charge:

> I am satisfied that if I had been able to get these men (left of his division) to do what I wanted, we would have captured a great many more than we did.
>
> **Question.** What was the difficulty?
>
> **Answer.** It was the want of proper discipline. Men get very much excited in battle; they are yelling, halloing, shooting, and unless they are very well drilled and disciplined, they do not wait for the orders of their colonels.
>
> **Question.** In the heat of the battle can a commanding officer have much control over his men?
>
> **Answer.** Not after the men become thoroughly engaged. But if men are well disciplined and accustomed to listen implicitly to the voice of their officers they can have an immense influence over them, if they (officers) stand by them and direct them. [113]

Non-Communication

One type of communication used in the Gettysburg campaign should be more appropriately classified as non-communication. In other words, when no information was received, it was a signal that nothing of interest had occurred and the operation would continue without changing the plan. This technique, however, was risky since it relied on unverifiable assumptions rather than the positive validation of information.

A specific case in point, at the beginning of the campaign, Gen. Lee gave instructions to his cavalry commander, Jeb Stuart: "It was expected that as soon as the Federal Army should cross the Potomac, General Stuart would give notice of its movements..."

Stuart, at this time was moving his cavalry force around the backside of the Union army. In the process of this rear action, communications were severed between Stuart and Lee. As a consequence, Stuart's silence intimated that the northern progress of enemy forces was behind schedule in keeping pace with the Army of Northern Virginia and Union forces were still south of the Potomac. Lee proceeded accordingly. He reported that "nothing having been heard from him [Stuart] since our entrance into Maryland, it was inferred that the enemy had not yet left Virginia...Orders were, therefore, issued to move upon Harrisburg." When the stunning news reached Lee that the Union army had already crossed the Potomac into Maryland and was close at hand, it forced the Army of Northern Virginia to concentrate and prepare for battle. [114]

Another example of lack of communication, perhaps one of convenience, involved the events leading up to Gen. Sickles' 3rd Corps forward move on July 2nd. According to Sickles, he was trying to locate Gen. Geary's former position near Little Round Top which, according to Gen. Meade, would have pinpointed part of the ground he was to occupy in the Union battle line. Sickles said, "I had no communication from Gen. Geary whatever. He had left the field, and there was no staff officer or representative of Gen. Geary to indicate his position, and for obvious reasons, because he was not in position."

Meade's version of the event conflicted with Sickles' account. Meade said:

> He sent to General Sickles a staff-officer with instructions to explain the position and its importance, and to ask, if troops could not be sent to relieve him, that General Sickles would send one of his staff to see the ground, and to place troops there on their arrival. He received for reply that General Sickles would attend to it in due time. No officer or troops came, and after waiting till his patience was exhausted General Geary withdrew and joined his corps. [115]

Conclusion

Command and communication frictions affected every level of command and every stage of the battle. Analyzing these frictions during the Gettysburg campaign point to several conclusions: 1. At the higher command levels, the Army of the Potomac experienced substantially more problems related to crossing spheres of command, the disadvantage of switching to a new commanding-general near the eve of battle, numerous other command changes and issues in understanding who was in charge at any one moment. 2. The Army of Northern Virginia entered the campaign with a trio of infantry corps commanders performing as a team for the first time. Its high command was, to a degree, put off balance by vagueness in important instructions or directions which lacked the detail desired by some commanders for expediting the intent of their commanding-general. 3. Both armies suffered deficiencies from substandard staff work and flawed communications. Such deficiencies were, with hindsight, often avoidable and had serious consequences to outcomes of operations. Frictions misdirected thousands of men out of the battle and forced thousands of others to retrace their march. Frictions placed soldiers in unintended, dangerous situations and caused unnecessary casualties. Frictions broke the string of solid victories for one army and brought another army perilously close to defeat.

We cannot place a measurable value of importance on the friction, mentioned in the beginning, regarding the pontoon boat shortage that prevented the Potomac crossing and delayed Union forces a day. It may be said that had that friction been averted another friction may well have been created because of an earlier crossing.

But it must be recognized that results of battles were determined by more factors than just manpower, terrain, or bullets and shells. Gunfire was only the final stage of settling an affair which began with the forced arrangement of men and weapons in attempts to achieve positions, better than those of the enemy, and lock their adversaries in battle to secure victory or prevent defeat. Command and communications were the two essentials functions necessary to orchestrate this crucial contest.

Frank G. Burke, Acting Archivist of the United States said, "Perhaps every generation must review history in terms of its own experience, not so much rewriting history as reinterpreting it through emphasis on topics not previously thought important." As a result, generations since have continuously re-molded events with conclusions and emphases quite different from the original versions. This work has attempted to provide a different perspective to understanding the complexities of the Gettysburg campaign; it was a sampler of just some of the types of command and communication frictions, important enough to sway the campaign's ultimate outcome.[116]

> "War is a special province of chance, and the gods of luck rise to full stature on the field of battle. Uncertainty and confusion are inseparable from combat: "Every action...only produces a

counteraction on the enemy's part, and the thousands of interlocking actions throw up millions of little frictions, accidents and chances, from which there emanates an all-embracing fog of uncertainty…the unknown is the first-born son of combat and uncertainty is its other self." [117]

Bibliography

Alexander, E. P., *Military Memoirs of a Confederate* [Charles Scribner's Sons, 1907]

Bandy, Freeland, & Bearss, eds., Samuel Stouffer, Arthur A. Lumsdaine, Marion Harper Lumsdaine, Robin M. Williams, Jr., M. Brewster Smith, Irving L. Janis, Shirley A. Star, Leonard S. Cottrell, Jr., *The American Soldier, Combat and its Aftermath* [Princeton, Princeton University Press, 1949], Vol. 2

Bandy, Freeland, & Bearss, *The Gettysburg Papers*, 2 Vols. (Morningside Bookshop, 1978)

Busey & Martin, *Regimental Strengths and Losses at Gettysburg*, Fourth edition, [Hightstown, N. J., Longstreet House, 2005]

Campbell, Eric, *Caldwell Clears the Wheatfield*, Gettysburg Magazine #3 [Morningside House, Inc., July, 1990]

Chamberlain, Joshua, *The Passing of the Armies* [Dayton, Morningside Bookshop, 1974]

Clausewitz, Carl von, *On War* [London, 1873, translation by J.J. Graham],[Internet Address: http://www.clausewitz.com/CWZHOME/On_War/BK1ch07.html]

Coddington, Edwin B., *The Gettysburg Campaign, a Study in Command* [New York, Charles Scribner's Sons, 1968]

DeTrobriand Regis, *FourYears with the Army of the Potomac*[Boston, Ticknor and Company, 1889]

Georg, Kathleen, *A Common Pride and Fame* [Gettysburg National Military Park]

Gordon, John B., *Reminiscences of the Civil War* [Reprint 1981, Time-Life Books, Inc.; New York, Charles Scribner's Sons, 1903]

Griffith, Paddy, *Battle Tactics of the Civil War* [Yale University Press,1989]

Hazlewood, Capt. M. W. "Pickett's Men in the Gettysburg Charge," *SHSP*, Vol. 23

Herbert, Walter H., *Fighting Joe Hooker*, [Lincoln, University of Nebraska Press, 1999]

Hoke, Jacob, *The Great Invasion* [New York, Thomas Yoseloff, New Edition, 1959]

Houghton Mifflin Company, *The American Heritage Dictionary of the English Language*, Fourth Edition [Houghton Mifflin Company 2000, 2004], Internet Address: http://www.answers.com/topic/chain-of-command

Johnson, Robert U. & Clarence C. Buel, eds., *Battles and Leaders of the Civil* War, [Century Company, 1884-89, Reprint, New York: Thomas Yoseloff, 1956], Vol. 3

Knight, Glenn B., editor and compiler, *Unofficial Dictionary for Marines* [Internet Address: http://4mermarine.com?USMC/dictionary.html copyright 2002-2005]

Ladd, David L. & Audrey J., eds., *The Bachelder Papers—Gettysburg in Their Own Words* [Dayton, Morningside House, Inc., 3 Vols: Vols. 1 & 2, 1994, Vol. 3, 1995.]

Martin, David G., *Gettysburg July 1* [Pennsylvania, Combined Books, 1995]

McLean, James L. Jr. & Judy W. , compilers, *Gettysburg Sources*, [Baltimore, Butternut and Blue], Vol. 1

Meade, George, *The Life and Letters of George Gordon Meade* [New York, Charles Scribner's Sons, 1913], Vol. 2

Muir, Rory, *Tactics and the Experience of Battle in the Age of Napoleon* [New Haven, Yale University Press, 1998]

Munden, Kenneth W. and Henry Putney Beers, *The Union, a Guide to Federal Archives Relating to the Civil War* (National Archives Trust Fund Board, 1986)

Nevins, Allan, ed., *A Diary of a Battle, The Personal Journals of Col. Charles S. Wainwright*
1861-1865 [Gettysburg, PA, Stan Clark Military Books, 1962 Reprint]

Norton, Oliver Willcox, *The Attack and Defense of Little Round Top* [Morningside Books, 1978]

Patterson, Grenny, McMillan, Switzler, *Crucial Conversations*, [New York, McGraw Hill, 2002]

Pfanz Harry,*Gettysburg, The Second Day* [Chapel Hill, The University of North Carolina Press, 1987]

Scheibert, Maj. of The Prussian Royal Engineers, Letter of November 21, 1877 from *Southern Historical Society Papers*, [Richmond, Va., February-March, 1883]

Stewart, George, *Pickett's Charge* [Greenwich CT, Fawcett Publications, Inc., 1963]

Trudeau, Noah Andre, *Civil War Times Illustrated*, October, 1991 issue

U. S. Govt., *Army of the Potomac,Report of the Joint Committee on the Conduct of the War* [Kraus Reprint Co., 1977], Part 2

U.S. War Department, *The War of the Rebellion: A Compilation of the Official Records of the Union and Confederate Armies*, 70 vols. In 128 parts, Series 1

Van Fleet, James K., *21 Days to Unlimited Power with People* [Englewood Cliffs, N.J., Prentice Hall, 1992]

Wiley, Bell Irvin, *The Life of Johnny Reb* [Louisiana University Press, 1978]

Notes: Introduction

[1] Carl von Clausewitz, *On War* [London, 1873, translation by J.J. Graham], Book 1, Chapter 7 [Internet Address: http://www.clausewitz.com/CWZHOME/On_War/BK1ch07.html]

[2] U.S. War Department, *The War of the Rebellion: A Compilation of the Official Records of the Union and Confederate Armies*, 70 vols. In 128 parts, Series 1, Vol. 27, Part 3, Page 228, Hereafter referred to as "*OR*, Vol.__, Part__, __." Unless noted, all references are from Series 1

[3] *The American Heritage® Dictionary of the English Language*, Fourth Edition Copyright © 2004, 2000 by Houghton Mifflin Company. Published by Houghton Mifflin Company [Internet Address: http://www.answers.com/topic/chain-of-command]; Glenn B. Knight, editor and compiler, *Unofficial Dictionary for Marines* [Internet Address: http://4mermarine.com?USMC/dictionary.html copyright 2002-2005]

[4] *OR*, Vol. 27, Part 1, 60

Part One - Command Frictions

[5] *OR*, Vol. 27, Part 3, 725

[6] *OR*, Vol. 27, Part 3, 747-48

[7] *OR*, Vol. 27, Part 3, 749

[8] *OR*, Vol. 27, Part 1, 55-57

[9] James L. McLean, Jr. & Judy W. Mclean, compilers, *Gettysburg Sources*, [Baltimore, Butternut and Blue], Vol. 1, 90

[10] *OR*, Vol. 27, Part 1, 735

[11] *OR*, Vol. 27, Part 1, 660

[12] Busey & Martin, *Regimental Strengths and Losses at Gettysburg*, Fourth edition, [Hightstown, N. J., Longstreet House, 2005], 16

[13] George Meade, *The Life and Letters of George Gordon Meade* [New York, Charles Scribner's Sons, 1913], Vol. 2, 3

[14] Noah Andre Trudeau, *Civil War Times Illustrated*, October, 1991 issue, 33; *The Life and Letters of George Gordon Meade*, Vol. 1, 367; Edwin B. Coddington, *The Gettysburg Campaign, a Study in Command* [New York, Charles Scribner's Sons, 1968], 235

[15] E. P. Alexander, *Military Memoirs of a Confederate* [Charles Scribner's Sons, 1907], 393

[16] Letter of November 21, 1877 from Maj. Scheibert, of The Prussian Royal Engineers, *Southern Historical Society Papers*, hereafter referred to as *SHSP*,[Richmond, Va., February-March, 1883],Vol. 5, 91

[17] Letter of November 21, 1877 from Maj. Scheibert, of The Prussian Royal Engineers, *SHSP*, Vol. 5, 91

[18] John B. Gordon, *Reminiscences of the Civil War* [Reprint 1981, Time-Life Books, Inc.; New York, Charles Scribner's Sons, 1903], 176

[19] *OR*, Vol. 27, Part 1, 47-48

[20] *OR*, Vol. 27, Part 1, 45, 47; *Fighting Joe Hooker*, Walter H. Herbert [Lincoln, University of Nebraska Press, 1999], 239

[21] Robert U. Johnson & Clarence C. Buel, eds., *Battles and Leaders of the Civil* War, hereafter referred to as *B & L*, 4 Vols. [Century Company, 1884-89, Reprint, New York: Thomas Yoseloff, 1956], Vol. 3 unless otherwise noted, 270; *Fighting Joe Hooker*, 247; Regis DeTrobriand, *FourYears with the Army of the Potomac*[Boston, Ticknor and Company, 1889], 518-19

[22] OR, Vol. 27, Part 1, 83-5, 92-3

[23] Rory Muir, *Tactics and the Experience of Battle in the Age of Napoleon* [New Haven, Yale University Press, 1998], 172; Bell Irvin Wiley, *The Life of Johnny Reb* [Louisiana University Press, 1978], 343

[24] Patterson, Grenny, McMillan, Switzler, *Crucial Conversations*, [New York, McGraw Hill, 2002], xii

[25] *OR*, Vol. 27, Part 1, 290

[26] *OR*, Vol. 27, Part 1, 544, 553-54

[27] *OR*, Vol. 27, Part 1, 155-68; *OR*, Vol. 27, Part 2, 283-91

[28] *OR*, Vol. 27, Part 1, 571

[29] *OR*, Vol. 27, Part 1, 244, 772, 765; *OR*, Vol. 27, Part 3, 533

[30] *OR*, Vol. 27, Part 1, 245-46 [Upon learning of Reynolds' death, Doubleday said: "The whole burden of the battle was thus suddenly thrown upon me," and "All this [action at the railroad cut] was accomplished in less than half an hour, and before General Howard had arrived on the field or assumed command."]

[31] David G. Martin, *Gettysburg July 1* [Pennsylvania, Combined Books, 1995], 180, 473-74

[32] *OR*, Vol. 27, Part 3, 463-64,466, 468
[33] *The Gettysburg Papers*, 2 Vols. (Morningside Bookshop, 1978), Vol. 2, 541-42
[34] *OR*, Vol. 27, Part 1, 704
[35] *OR*, Vol. 27, Part 1,
[36] *OR*, Vol. 27, Part 1, 704, 759
[37] *OR*, Vol. 27, Part 1, 542
[38] Harry Pfanz, *Gettysburg, The Second Day* [Chapel Hill, The University of North Carolina Press, 1987], 173
[39] *OR*, Vol. 27, Part 1, 769-70
[40] *OR*, Vol. 27, Part 1. 780, [In his report Gen. Ruger, temporary division commander under Gen. Williams, who was 12th corps' acting commander, referred to Slocum as "commanding right of main line"; Coddington's *The Gettysburg Campaign*, 314, mentions Slocum as being "in charge of the right wing."]
[41] James K. Van Fleet, *21 Days to Unlimited Power with People* [Englewood Cliffs, N.J.,Prentice Hall, 1992], 10-11, 105-106

Part 2: Communication Frictions

[42] *Crucial Conversations*, xi
[43] *OR*, Vol. 25, Part 2, 786-87
[44] *Army of the Potomac,Report of the Joint Committee on the Conduct of the War* [Kraus Reprint Co., 1977], Part 2, 469
[45] *Gettysburg, The Second Day*, 407-08
[46] Eric Campbell, *Caldwell Clears the Wheatfield*, Gettysburg Magazine #3 [Morningside House, Inc., July, 1990], 33-34; *Gettysburg, The Second Day*, 519-20
[47] *OR*, Vol. 27, Part 1, 883-84
[48] Allan Nevins,ed., *A Diary of a Battle, The Personal Journals of Col. Charles S. Wainwright*
1861-1865 [Gettysburg, PA, Stan Clark Military Books, 1962 Reprint], 252-53
[49] *OR,* Vol. 11, Part 3, 40
[50] David L. & Audrey J. Ladd, eds., *The Bachelder Papers— Gettysburg in Their Own Words*, Hereafter referred to as *BP*, [Dayton, Morningside House, Inc., 3 Vols: Vols. 1 & 2, 1994, Vol. 3, 1995.], Vol. 1, 426-7
[51] *BP*, Vol. 2, 791, 795
[52] *BP*, Vol. 1, 443-44
[53] *BP*, Vol. 1, 379-80

[54] *The Gettysburg Campaign, a Study in Command*, 448-49; Paddy Griffith, *Battle Tactics of the Civil War* [Yale University Press,1989], 62
[55] Letter of November 21, 1877 from Maj. Scheibert, of The Prussian Royal Engineers, *SHSP*, Vol. 5, 91
[56] *Battle Tactics of the Civil War*, 55; *OR*, Series 4, Vol. 2, 593
[57] Jacob Hoke, *The Great Invasion* [New York, Thomas Yoseloff, New Edition, 1959], 34-5, 40
[58] *OR*, Series 4, Vol. 2, 950
[59] *The Gettysburg Papers*, 544
[60] *The Gettysburg Papers*, 550
[61] *Gettysburg, The Second Day*, 323-4
[62] *OR*, Series 4, Vol. 2, 950
[63] *Military Memoirs of a Confederate*, 378
[64] *Battles and Leaders of the Civil* War, 305
[65] *21 Days to Unlimited Power with People*, 127,129, 131, 133, 137, 139
[66] Rory Muir, *Tactics and the Experience of Battle in the Age of Napoleon* [New Haven, Yale University Press, 1998], 148
[67] *B & L*, 411
[68] *BP*, Vol. 2, 1096
[69] Joshua Chamberlain, *The Passing of the Armies* [Dayton, Morningside Bookshop, 1974], 98-9
[70] *OR*, Vol. 27, Part 1, 45-47
[71] *OR*, Vol. 27, Part 1, 49
[72] *BP*, Vol. 1, 215
[73] *OR*, Vol. 27, Part 1, 826
[74] *Regimental Strengths and Losses at Gettysburg*, 94
[75] *Regimental Strengths and Losses at Gettysburg*, 93
[76] *OR*, Vol. 27, Part 2, 614
[77] *OR*, Vol. 27, Part 2,444
[78] *OR*, Vol. 27, Part 2, 318,555, 607
[79] *OR*, Vol. 27, Part 2, 555
[80] *OR*, Vol. 27, Part 2, 317-18
[81] *OR*, Vol. 27, Part 1, 592; *The Gettysburg Campaign, a Study in Command*, 399
[82] *OR*, Vol. 27, Part 3, 519
[83] *OR*, Vol. 27, Part 3, 567
[84] *OR*, Vol. 27, Part 3, 558, 562, 567
[85] *BP*, Vol. 2, 927

[86] George R. Stewart, *Pickett's Charge* [Boston, Houghton Mifflin Company, 1987], 111

[87] *Pickett's Charge*, 114

[88] *Reminiscences of the Civil War*, 155, *B & L*, 445

[89] *Military Memoirs of a Confederate*, 18

[90] *B & L*, 345

[91] *The Life and Letters of George Gordon Meade*, 71

[92] *The Great Invasion*, 421; Capt. M. W. Hazlewood, "Pickett's Men in the Gettysburg Charge," *SHSP*, Vol. 23, 232

[93] *OR*, Vol. 27, Part 1, 67-68

[94] *OR*, Vol. 27, Part 2, 697

[95] *OR*, Vol. 27, Part 1, 74, 78

[96] *The Passing of the Armies*, 96

[97] *Battle Tactics of the Civil War*, 11

[98] *Pickett's Charge*, 168

[99] Oliver Willcox Norton, *The Attack and Defense of Little Round Top* [Morningside Books, 1978], 32

[100] Kathleen Georg, *A Common Pride and Fame* [Gettysburg National Military Park], Part 3, Appendix A, 426

[101] *OR*, Vol. 27, Part 1, 222

[102] The Great Invasion, 450

[103] Maureen Burke, manager of training, Coca-Cola Enterprises, Inc., *Crucial Conversations*, i

[104] *OR*, Vol. 27, Part 1, 628; Details of how this took place vary but the fact that it happened from a misunderstood order is central to the point.

[105] *BP*, Vol. 1, 193-94

[106] *BP*, Vol. 1, 364-65, see also *OR*, Vol. 27, Part 1, 781

[107] *OR*, Vol. 27, Part 2, 368

[108] *B & L*, 335

[109] *OR*, Vol. 27, Part 1, 611

[110] *OR*, Vol. 27, Part 1, 356-57

[111] *Battle Tactics of the Civil War*, 62

[112] *Battle Tactics of the Civil War*, 62

[113] *Army of the Potomac,Report of the Joint Committee on the Conduct of the War,* Part 2, 443

[114] *OR*, Vol. 27, Part 2, 316

[115] *B & L*, 414, 419

[116] Kenneth W. Munden and Henry Putney Beers, *The Union, a Guide to Federal Archives Relating to the Civil War* (National Archives Trust Fund Board, 1986), Foreword, iv

[117] Bandy, Freeland, & Bearss, eds., Samuel Stouffer, Arthur A. Lumsdaine, Marion Harper Lumsdaine, Robin M. Williams, Jr., M. Brewster Smith, Irving L. Janis, Shirley A. Star, Leonard S. Cottrell, Jr., *The American Soldier, Combat and its Aftermath* [Princeton, Princeton University Press, 1949], Vol. 2, 83

Index

Ackerman, Capt. Andrew, 32
Aiken, D. Wyatt, 85
Alexander, Col. E. P. 20, 74-5, 77
Anderson, Maj. Gen. Richard H., 65
Ayres, Brig. Gen. Romeyn, 29

Baldwin, Col. Clark, 83
Benedict, Lt. G. G., 16
Birney, Maj. Gen. David, 41-2, 47, 70, 82
Bootes, Capt. Levi C., 29
Buford, Brig. Gen. John, 35, 41, 66,76
Burling, Col. George, 32-3, 35
Butterfield, Maj. Gen. Daniel, 6, 51, 60, 79

Cadwalader, Brig. Gen. George, 23
Caldwell, Brig. Gen. John, 48, 69
Carr, Brig. Gen. Joseph, 38, 83
chain of command, 10-2, 14-5, 17-19, 23, 25-7, 29, 34, 36, 43, 45-46, 48-9, 60, 80
Chamberlain, Col. Joshua, 62, 79
changed style, 19, 43
changes in the chain of command, 17
command changes, 17-18, 29, 32, 35-6, 39-40, 42-3, 89
command continuity, 19
communication:
- speed, 79
- distance, 80-82

communicator style, 58
conflicting orders, 4, 67
continuity, 17-19, 43-4
corps commands, 34
Couch, Maj. Gen. Darius, 11-2, 14, 78
Coulter, Col. Richard, 29
Crawford, Brig. Gen. Samuel, 15,47,49
cutoff communication, 77

Day, Col. Hannibal, 29
DeTrobriand, Col. Regis, 24
discipline to follow orders, 86
discretionary orders, 72-74
disregarded orders, 65
Dobke, Colonel Adolphus, 16
Doubleday, Maj. Gen. Abner, 33-4, 36, 38, 41, 55,61, 86

Early, Maj. Gen. Jubal, 57, 67, 72-3, 78, 79
Eckert, Maj., 79
encryption Problems, 79
Ewell, Lt. Gen. Richard, 21, 28, 42, 66-9, 72-5

failed notification, 76
familiarity, 18, 26-8, 44
Fasset, Capt., 47-8
French, Maj. Gen. William, 42, 70
functions of command and communication, 8, 81-2

Geary, Brig. Gen. John, 64, 88
General Order #68, 70
Gibbon, Brig. Gen. John, 41, 87
Gordon, Brig. Gen. John, 22

Halleck, Maj. Gen. Henry, 12, 14-15, 22-5, 62-3, 70-1, 78-9
Hancock, Maj. Gen. Winfield, 36-8, 40-1, 47, 49-50, 74, 77
Haupt, Brig. Gen. Hermann, 23
Hazard, Capt. John, 50
Heintzelman, Maj. Gen. Samuel, 11, 14-5
Hildebrandt, Maj. Hugo, 47, 49

Hill, Lt. Gen. A. P., 28, 42, 46, 65-68, 77
Hood, Maj. Gen. John, 39
Hooker, Maj. Gen. Joseph, 11, 13-16, 18-20, 22-4, 29, 41, 44, 58, 62-3, 69, 77
Howard, Maj. Gen. O. O. Howard, 34, 36-8, 40-2, 55
Humphreys, Brig. Gen. Andrew, 33
Hunt, Brig. Gen. Henry, 49-51, 54, 58
Ingalls, Brig. Gen. Rufus, 51, 82

Jackson, Lt. Gen. Thomas, 21, 27-8

Kearny, Maj. Philip J., 33
Kershaw, Brig. Gen. Joseph, 84-5

lack of notification, 39
Law, Brig. Gen. Evander, 39
Lee, Gen. Robert E., 7-8, 13, 15, 19-25, 27-8, 32, 42-44, 46, 54, 56-58, 60, 65-9, 71-9, 87-8
Leonard, Col. Samuel, 29
Lincoln, Abraham, 23-4, 70-1
Lloyd, Capt. William, 32
Lockwood, Brig. Gen. Henry, 12
Logan, Capt. Doraster, 32
Longstreet, Lt. Gen. James, 21, 27-28, 57, 62, 65, 74-5, 77
Lyle, Col. Peter, 29

manpower, 82
Martin, Capt. A. P., 17
Martin, Capt. Luther, 32
McAllister, Capt. R., 32
McGilvery, Lt. Col. Freeman, 49-50, 64
Meade, Maj. Gen. George, 11-2, 16, 18-21, 24-9, 32, 34-41, 43-4, 47, 50-1, 54-5, 58-61, 69-74, 76, 77-9, 81-2, 88
Melton, Maj. Samuel, 53, 56

message:
corruption/misunderstood orders, 82
poor or incorrect wording, 69
origination, 60
Moore, Capt. of Gen. Meade's staff 47

Newton, Maj. Gen. John, 41
non-communication, 87
Norton, Capt. L. B. 51, 80

O'Rorke, Col. Patrick, 27-8, 81
Order of Battle, 32
Orders with Difficult Prerequisites, 69

Paul, Brig. Gen. Gabriel, 29
Peeples, Lt. Samuel, 47
Pendleton, Brig. Gen. William, 53, 58, 77
personal relationships, 22
Pettigrew, Brig. Gen. James, 66, 74, 81
Pickett, Maj. Gen. George, 74-7, 81, 87
Pleasonton, Maj. Gen. Alfred, 51, 76
Prescott, Col. George, 85-6
protocol, 10, 45-9

Rafferty, Col. Thomas, 37, 54-5
Reynolds, Maj. Gen. John, 33-6, 40-2, 73
Rodes, Maj. Gen. Robert, 57, 66-7
Root, Col. Adrian, 29
Rowley, Brig. Gen. Thomas, 36
Ruger, Brig. Gen. Thomas, 84

Scheibert, Maj. Justus, 20
Schenck, Maj. Gen. Robert, 12, 14
Schenck, 12, 14-5, 62, 78
Schoonover, Lt. John, 32
Schurz, Maj. Gen. Carl, 42

Sedgwick, Maj. Gen. John, 33-4, 42, 71
senior commander on the field, 33, 35-6, 41-2
seniority, 11
seniority protocol, 10,33, 35, 37, 40
Sickles, Maj. Gen. Daniel, 17, 20, 27, 36-38, 41, 47, 48, 54-5, 64, 69-70, 76-7, 88
Slocum, Maj. Gen. Henry, 33-4, 36-42, 47, 50, 59, 63, 84
Slough, Brig. Gen. John, 15
Smith, Brig. Gen. W. F. 12
spheres of command, 13, 16, 35, 88
staff, 25-6, 28, 35, 40, 46, 51, 53-9, 64, 70, 72, 76, 88-9
staff communication, 51
Stahel, Maj. Gen. Julius, 11
Stanton, Edwin, 11, 23
Stuart, Maj. Gen. J. E. B., 21, 56, 75, 77-8, 87-8
Sweitzer, Col. Jacob, 85
Sykes, Maj. Gen. George, 29, 42, 47, 69-70, 81, 83

transmitting orders verbally, 61
Tremain, Maj. Henry, 48
Trimble, Maj. Gen. Isaac, 72-4, 81
Turnbull, Capt. Charles, 6
Tyler, Brig. Gen. Robert, 63

uncertain instructions, 62
unfamiliarity, 27

von Clausewitz, 6, 10

Wainright, Col. Charles, 36, 86
Warren, Brig. Gen. Gouverneur, 27-8, 54, 62, 71, 81
Welch, Lt. Col. Norval, 82
Williams, Brig. Gen. Alpheus, 34, 39, 40, 42, 63-4
wing commanders, 32-34, 43
wing commands, 33-4, 39
Zook, Brig. Gen. Samuel, 48-9

ABOUT THE AUTHOR

Philip M. Cole was born and raised in Gettysburg, Pennsylvania. He is one of ten children. The family has a history of military tradition – he was one of the seven of nine sons who served. In the Civil War, his ancestors were members of the 76th Pennsylvania Infantry, the Keystone Zouaves, and involved in such battles as Fort Wagner and Cold Harbor.

After receiving a Bachelor of Science degree in accounting from Pennsylvania State University, he was a regional control manager for an international corporation. He founded a marketing firm. He lives near Gettysburg, works as a licensed battlefield guide at Gettysburg National Military Park, and is the author of *Civil War Artillery at Gettysburg*.

Colecraft Industries
970 Mt. Carmel Road
Orrtanna, Pennsylvania, 17353

colecraftbooks@aol.com

Printed in the United States
97698LV00002B/41/A